MANAGE TO SELL YOUR BUSINESS

WEALTH CREATION SECRETS OF THE PROS

ROBERT W. SCARLATA

ISBN: 1470199270
ISBN-13: 9781470199272

Library of Congress Control Number: 2012904223
CreateSpace, North Charleston, SC

CONTENTS

Exhibits

Company Life Cycle
Readiness Matrix
Strategies for Maximizing Value: Typical PEGs vs. Typical Business Owners
Chart 1: Widget Mfg. Co., Inc., Summary of EBITDA
Chart 2: Widget Mfg. Co., Inc., Income Statement Summary
Chart 3: Widget Mfg. Co., Inc., Balance Sheet Summary
Chart 4: Widget Mfg. Co., Inc., Internal Rate of Return Analysis
Chart 5: Widget Mfg. Co., Inc., Purchase Analysis
Maslow's Hierarchy of Needs

DEDICATION

To Rhonda, for your unwavering support.

ACKNOWLEDGMENTS

In writing this book, I've drawn from a lifetime of experiences and associations with so many individuals who provided inspiration and assistance—beginning with my grandfather, who was the first entrepreneur I ever knew. My parents, Bea and Bob, always encouraging, endowed me with strong self-esteem and the belief that I could achieve anything I set my mind to. Jeff Davidson, my good friend and a superlative writer/speaker, made this book possible: he was instrumental in developing its form and narrative, and without him the book would most likely never have existed. My long-term associate George Gifford has been an inspiration since 1992. George "never met an idea he didn't like," and following his risk-taking example made it relatively easy for me to set off to write my first book. Recently we joined a national exit planning group called Pinnacle Equity Solutions, and new concepts in a book by its founder, John Leonetti, have enriched this text in multiple ways. Some of the analysis and charts were prepared by Richard Scarlata. Leslie Bell assisted in refining my thoughts and efforts. I'd also like to thank my/our many clients over the years. I have learned something from every single one of you. Last but not least, the professionals interviewed for this book reinforced the message in a way only those who have lived these experiences can appreciate.

FOREWORD

In *Manage to Sell Out: Wealth Creation Secrets of the Pros,* Robert Scarlata covers ground like few other authors have and offers keen insights to small business owners with potential to sell their companies for many multiples of their investment.

Scarlata's premise is that private equity groups (PEGs) are prospective sellers from day one and that this is the critical component of their business model in acquiring companies for their investment portfolio. The end goal is to sell the company for many orders of magnitude of the owner's equity investment. Because PEGs maintain this singular focus, they are able to achieve three, four, and five times' return on their investment equity upon resale compared to that which the typical middle market private business owner would likely be able to achieve. In this regard, this book is a revelation to business owners, each of whom know that one day, one way or the other, they will have to exit their business.

Manage to Sell Out is not, however, a "how-to" book, although much how-to information is provided. Rather, it's a "here's-what" book, and the distinction is vital. How-to books are suitable for readers who already know the challenges they face and who seek information on how to surmount them. Good how-to books provide step-by-step plans for achieving particular goals.

The process of selling one's business, however, involves so many steps that it's not practical to cover everything a small business owner needs to do to prepare the business for an acquisition.

There are intermediary firms, whose roles are explained in this book, that do that spectacularly well. *Manage to Sell Out* says to business owners, "You might never have even heard of PEGs, but for all the time and effort you've put into your business, it makes sense to be aware of who PEGs are, how they're structured, what they do, and why they succeed. It's supremely important to know how they can benefit you and your business." Thus, this book for some will represent a revelation.

Manage to Sell Out is among the best books of its kind because it offers in everyday terms, with a candidness that is refreshing, an inside look the world of PEGs, the potential interest they might have in your business, the key steps in preparing your business for acquisition, and your options once your business is acquired. As such, this book can make a difference when it comes to cashing in some or all of your chips for an extraordinary return, achieving or maintaining the lifestyle you've always dreamed about, and seeing your business succeed several notches above where you are now.

What's more, this book will benefit you in many ways, even if you haven't been contemplating the exit or sale of your business, and especially if you haven't heard of PEGs. Unlike many small business guides that have been circulating for years, *Manage to Sell Out* identifies what it takes to raise the value of your business, not just by 5 percent to 25 percent but by 200 percent to even 400 percent. So, you're in for an extraordinary read. I envy you for the adventure upon which you are about to embark.

Jeff Davidson

PREFACE

Business owners live their businesses 24/7. During waking hours, and often in their dreams, they're thinking about their businesses. Business owners often take great risks. Nearly all those I've met in my twenty-six years marketing and selling businesses—and that would be thousands—have a story about nearly not making payroll or other severe difficulties they faced at one time or another.

And so I've written this book with the goal in mind of helping business owners reap their due desserts. Nearly every client has said at one time or another, "I don't want to leave anything on the table." In other words, I want full value for my business, for the risks I've taken, for the profit engine I've created.

Too often, however, we've found that mistakes have been made—whether by omission or commission, it doesn't matter. Those mistakes cost clients hundreds or thousands of dollars, on several occasions reaching into the seven figures. For one reason or another, the owner was not aware of the implications of his or her decisions.

I've written this book to provide business owners with some modicum of experience that may help them avoid those costly mistakes or to take steps to maximize their eventual financial outcome... plain and simple.

Introduction: Secrets of Wealth Creation

Here's the good news:

Many entrepreneurs just like you have retired **rich**.

After founding, running, and building their mid-sized companies—and devoting a lifetime of money, blood, sweat, and tears—they sold them for the **full value** of all they had invested. Imagine their surprise and delight when they received a payout that greatly exceeded not only their expectations but sometimes their wildest dreams.

Here's the bad news:

Many entrepreneurs just like you **could have retired rich but didn't**.

Some didn't know the steps they needed to take—or the costs of failing to take them. Some lacked discipline—they knew what they need to do but kept doing what was easier or more fun instead. And some didn't have a coherent strategy—they got caught up in the everyday tasks of running a business instead of pursuing an effective long-term plan. Many entrepreneurs have the capability to maximize the value of their companies but, sadly, will never realize anywhere near the return they could achieve. Imagine the heartbreak when a company's high potential value has been compromised by defects in management or strategy, when a business owner realizes, "If I had just done things a little differently, I could have sold this company for a whole lot more."

I'm a partner in a company that specializes in the valuation and sale of privately held, middle-market companies such as yours. We're often called "intermediaries." Our objective is to maximize our clients' after-tax net. Over the past twenty-five years, my partners and I have participated in the sale of more than four hundred small and medium-sized businesses throughout the country, valued from $70,000 to $79 million.

However, in our work, we've also seen many owners who could have achieved greater-than-expected wealth in a sale—but instead shot themselves in the foot. Why? What do business owners do that prevents them from achieving the optimal payoff for all the years they've invested and risked in their business? Well, in many cases the defects are similar. And they all come down to one thing: **not fully understanding the strategies for building equity in a company—as perceived by the buyers or potential prospects for that company.** You'd never sell your products or services without understanding what your customers want. The same goes for your company: to maximize value, you have to know what they want.

That's why I wrote this book: to help you avoid the pitfalls and take the vital steps necessary to maximize the value of your business. In our dealings with business owners, we have seen from top to bottom what works and what does not. Thus, the information I present in *Manage to Sell Out* is time-tested and proven. In this book, you will:

- Learn why it's imperative to always be prepared to sell your company, even if you aren't planning to exit your business.

- Discover what private equity groups, or PEGs, are, what they do, and how they earn tremendous returns.

- Identify the offensive strategies that build wealth and the defensive strategies that help minimize risks to your business and your personal equity.

- Uncover the differences between the way PEGs and private businesses operate, and how to emulate PEG practices in operating your business and preparing it for sale.

- Learn the crucial steps to selling your business, including recasting your financial statements to reflect your business's true value to a purchaser.

- Determine how to protect your interests, your assets, and your family in a sale.

- Explore the many options available to you after you sell your business.

Manage to Sell Out will help you navigate the process of maximizing value in today's challenging business climate. I have crafted this book so that it is brief and to the point, because I know you don't have the time or energy to read a voluminous tome. I deliver the message to you as succinctly as is practical, with some stories, many case histories, and interviews with principals within the field. I rely on graphics and bullet points because I know you like information that is quick and easy to digest. Wherever I discuss dollar amounts, these are 100 percent accurate, based on actual case histories. **You will find no hyperbole, exaggeration, grandiose claims, or spin.**

Once you finish this book, you'll have a good understanding of what is required to generate more wealth from your company than you might have presumed possible. The insights presented here will help you increase your personal equity not just by 5 or 10 percent but by an order or orders of magnitude: potentially **many times more** than you otherwise might receive. This is precisely what the "pros" do when they acquire privately owned middle-market companies, just like yours. If this seems far-fetched, then you are precisely the right reader for this book. It could prove be a game changer—even a life changer—for you.

However, let me emphasize that this book is no substitute for professional assistance in selling your company (only when you and it are ready...and it's imperative as to the preparedness for both). Several aspects of preparing a business for acquisition are sufficiently complex that they could merit entire books on their own. The longer you've been in business and the more facets your business has, the more complicated selling it will be. That's why it's critical to have expertise in a variety of different disciplines, such as finance, accounting, business law, marketing, and business operations, as well as an understanding of the specific industry in which your business operates. The vast majority of business owners do not have this range of expertise, but excellent intermediaries do—for more on this, see Chapter 6.

You *can* generate wealth from the sale of your business—wealth that can exceed your highest expectations. So, let's get started.

Chapter 1: To Sell, or Not to Sell—That is the Question

If you've picked up this book, you're probably thinking about the future, a future in which you are no longer the sole owner of your business. But you might not be ready—emotionally or practically speaking—to sell. This chapter will help you see that you should always be ready, whether you actually sell or not. Being prepared to do so is the best strategy for optimizing the current management of your business.

It will also help you think through the benefits of selling or partnering with another firm, such as a private equity group or PEG.

We Get It: You're Attached to Your Business

For a variety of reasons, many business founders are hardwired to believe that they alone can lead their venture to sterling success:

- **It's theirs.** After all, they had the initial idea and impetus to launch the venture. They are the ones who've been with the company every step of the way. Their experience, methods, and mindset permeate every aspect of the business.

- **It's them.** Typically, business owners' self-worth is intimately connected with their business. Consciously or subconsciously, the business is viewed as an extension of the business owner's psyche. Business owners certainly do not consider their businesses mere investments. In addition, because business owners are often psychologically as well as financially invested in their businesses, the 24/7, day-to-day operations can obscure and blind the owner to opportunities elsewhere that might be more lucrative and fulfilling.

- **They are naturally enthusiastic and optimistic.** In landmark study in the February 28 *Harvard Business Review,* Harvard Business School associate professor Noam Wasserman says this: "New ventures are usually labors of love for entrepreneurs, and they become emotionally attached" to their ventures. Perhaps this explains why many founding entrepreneurs are naive about the issues that confront them and are overconfident about both their short-term and long-term potential. Slightly more than 80 percent of founders Wasserman studied believed that they would succeed in their chosen line of business (although less than 60 percent of business founders actually do). Moreover, 33 percent of founders believed that the odds of their own success were 100 percent. "Like the passing of distinguished individuals," writes Michael Hitzik in *The Los Angeles Times,* "the passing of great corporations should prompt us to ponder the transience of earthly glory." To think that your small company isn't vulnerable when Blue Chip companies like Kodak are going bankrupt is folly and a substantial weakness vis-à-vis protecting and defending your personal and family wealth.

- **They have a lot to lose.** Founders are also motivated by fear of loss. Virtually every business owner has family or friends who have failed in business, or knows of someone who has suffered substantial financial losses. At the same time, most business owners have developed a certain lifestyle and have a spouse who has become used to that lifestyle. Since the business owner's personal net worth is typically tied up in the business, the family depends on the business enterprise to sustain them in the manner to which they have become accustomed.

Moreover, because banks and lending institutions treat small businesses as proprietorships—even when the business is incorporated or is in a legal partnership—most small businesses have to personally sign guarantees for any debt that they incur. Thus, small business owners are predisposed to avoid taking certain steps they view as too risky, even when they involve significant business opportunities. The fear of losing what they have already acquired trumps their willingness to take advantage of potentially lucrative sources of new business revenues.

WHO WILL RUN YOUR BUSINESS FOREVER? (HINT: NOT YOU)

We understand why you, as a successful middle-market business owner, might be very reluctant to sell your company or take on investors or partners, especially because you will almost certainly then take on a diminished role in your company. But there's no getting around it: someday, someone else will run your company. As the saying goes, "Life is what happens when you're making other plans." Business owners are no different than anyone else in at least one respect: they are not going to live forever. One way or another, someday the business they have built will no longer belong to them. **Owners have a host of reasons for selling their business, but at some point each will cash in his or her chips. If you can cash yours in while they have substantial value, thus preserving and diversifying your net worth, why wouldn't you?** Helping you realize this potential is the whole purpose of this book.

Many owners sell because they want to. Maybe they aren't having fun anymore; maybe they are no longer working well with a partner. We've often seen situations where partners who had operated harmoniously for years can no longer get along. They may have disagreed on an important issue or series of issues. Whatever the reason, squabbling partners can become a major obstacle to the well-being of a company. Most often, though, owners who sell because they want to are looking to cash out or take some chips off the table, retire early, or do something different.

Often, however, owners sell because they have to. Health and age are common reasons. Either the owner is not physically able to run the business anymore, cannot run it at the capacity required, or doesn't enjoy running it at diminished capacity. Some owners are beset by family illness, and some are simply burned out after years of running a business 24/7. If the business has an heir apparent (say a child of the owner or a key employee), great. If not, the owner may need to prepare the company for sale just at the moment when this may be the most difficult thing to do.

And this is key: if you've waited too long and you're in a have-to-sell position, you're inevitably going to leave money on the table. In particular, owners who get burned out and have to sell sometimes end up with a fraction of what they could have realized. Thereafter, their life experience is markedly different than what it could have been if they'd had a strategic plan for selling the business. When you get to the have-to-sell stage, you have put yourself at a great disadvantage.

We liken a business to a train with several cars. The owner represents the engine. If that engine loses its spark and isn't excited about the business, creativity can decline. Unfortunately, like a train, when a business begins to slide backwards down the hill, it's usually not a slow and even descent—it can be an unstoppable rush off a cliff. So, even if you currently believe you're not ready to sell your business, you will want to think about it sooner rather

4

than later. The message, the point, is: be prepared to sell at all times, even if you have no intent of selling, taking chips off the table, or finding a partner now.

ALL COMPANIES ARE PERISHABLE

Like people, companies and industries are mortal, especially now. We live in a society where the domestic and world economies are shifting at an ever-accelerating rate. This rapid pace of change dramatically shortens the stages of a company's growth, shown in the illustration at right.

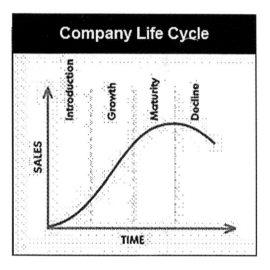

The typical company begins with introduction, experiences growth, reaches maturity, and eventually declines. Today, the interval for each of these business phases is becoming shorter. Competition is increasing, and obsolescence is occurring at a faster pace. Some companies, like Apple for example, deal with the fact that their products will eventually become outmoded through "creative obsolescence" and its corollary "creative destruction"—by being the ones to create the next new thing. Many more companies, however, are not able to reinvent themselves over and over and need to be prepared to sell while they are on the upswing.

The number one rule in properly positioning a company for sale is to **make your deal while the company is still growing**. No one can predict when growth will plateau. Any time the company is experiencing growth represents a potentially good time to sell it.

This might seem counterintuitive, but the reason most buyers are in the market is the opportunity to grow an enterprise and earn a higher rate of return on their investment. If a business has already reached a plateau, the returns that potential buyers can realize are limited. At this point, you may be milking the company for a return on your investment. However, that return on investment, as a percentage, will not grow significantly.

Worse, when you stop growing, the number of prospective buyers diminishes. You want there to be competition for the purchase of your business—a bidding war, so to speak. This most likely occurs when you are still in a growth mode. Fewer prospective buyers translates into an anemic sale price in a limited auction.

As we'll discuss further in Chapter 2, private equity groups pay premiums for companies that are poised for growth. It's that simple. Companies that have demonstrated little growth thus far will still be highly attractive if they are positioned for greater growth. Businesses are dynamic enterprises, and what owner or investor can safely predict what's going to happen tomorrow? Within certain industries and particular niches, however, opportunities for growth can be both recognizable and achievable.

Business owners often don't think in these terms, to their extreme disadvantage. We've seen that a moment too late can be an eternity too late. A business is no different than any other asset. **It has a shelf life, a sell-by date.** If you don't sell the asset while it's hot, you're likely never again to have the opportunity to sell it at that price.

AN OFFER TOO GOOD TO REFUSE

If someone came to you today and made you a reasonable offer for your company, would you be prepared to take it? If you were not, you would have in essence **bought the company back for the value**

of that offer. Would you be comfortable with that knowledge? If something were to happen that caused the value of the business to decline, would you be kicking yourself later? I know I would.

And there are many things that can cause the value of a business to decline.

Unexpected turns of events. Looking at the US economy, who could have predicted that turmoil in the subprime mortgage industry would threaten the world's largest automotive manufacturer, General Motors? Humankind's base of knowledge doubles every five years. No company today, large or small, enjoys any guarantees. It is foolhardy to believe that any business, from General Motors on down, is completely secure. But entrepreneurs in particular suffer from this form of self-delusion. As with entire industries, thanks to external circumstances, sometimes a business can be wiped out overnight. Events impacting an industry can be cyclical or random. One-time events are the hardest to predict and most difficult to manage.

Here's an example from one of our clients: Wood is used in many industries, but it eventually wears out and periodically has to be replaced. Our client derived a third of its revenues from collecting and reselling used wood as fuel for an energy-regeneration plant. However, the used industrial wood was infused with a toxic preservative that becomes airborne upon burning. Suddenly, a new EPA regulation dictated this practice had to stop. The regeneration plants to which our client sold did not possess the specially equipped filters needed to eliminate the airborne toxins. With this single regulation, our client's projected revenue for the coming year decreased by 33 percent. Worse, the buyer we had painstakingly sought, found, and won over for our client withdrew within days.

Black swans. Many small business owners and executives are well aware of the term "black swan"—meaning a large-scale, unexpected, catastrophic event. Over the past several decades, a number of black swans have occurred internationally, nationally, and regionally. These include terrorist strikes, currency devaluations, hurricanes, floods, earthquakes, and other man-made, economic, and natural disasters.

We represented a software company that was about to sell for $11 million to a $300 million company in the same industry. As the subprime mortgage debacle intensified, the board of directors for the potential acquiring company put all acquisitions on hold, stating that they had lost the ability to predict future revenues. You can wait weeks or months, but once a potential acquisition is delayed, the odds of the sale going through decline with each passing day. Our client lost the huge sale he had been counting on, and we ended up expending considerable time, money, and effort all for naught.

In 2008, clients of ours who had successful businesses in energy development were hit hard when oil prices dropped from one hundred fifty dollars a barrel to thirty-five dollars a barrel, while their break-even point was seventy dollars a barrel. I could recount such scenarios over and over again. Whether it's a federal regulation, the subprime fiasco, an economic downturn, 9/11, or Hurricane Katrina, black swan events occur again and again.

In my view, the speed of change today increases a business owner's risk in the face of black swans. We're going to see more and more black swans, not fewer. The revolutions going on in the Middle East, for example, will have all kinds of ramifications for small business owners for years to come. Will this regime or that take over? Will the new regime nationalize the oil fields? Will tourism fall?

Domestically, do increased budget deficits mean increased taxes? Many people believe so. Does that ultimately translate into a higher discount rate to buy a company, which means lower selling prices? Many different factors, locally, nationally, and globally, can impact business, and no one anywhere is able to make sense of it all.

An axiom of the insurance industry is, "If you can't afford to lose it, you need to insure it." The corollary for small business owners is, "When you have the opportunity to sell your business, you need to jump at the chance." When you've earned enough and reached a certain vantage point, you need to consider the possibility of losing the opportunity to sell for maximum value, not to mention incurring declines in your equity.

The summary to all of these observations is succinct: when it comes to generating wealth, the old axiom "strike while the iron is hot" is the best financial advice you might ever receive.

The psychology of immunity. What is it about business and life that makes us believe we are immune from the same hazards and misfortunes as others? Perhaps we're wired that way and the notion is a prime factor for survival.

> *When anyone asks me how I can best describe my experience in nearly forty years at sea, I merely say, uneventful. Of course there have been winter gales, and storms and fog and the like. But in all my experience, I have never been in any accident...or any sort worth speaking about. I have seen but one vessel in distress in all my years at sea. I never saw a wreck and never have been wrecked nor was I ever in any predicament that threatened to end in disaster of any sort.*
>
> *—Edward J. Smith, 1907*
> *(future Captain of the RMS Titanic, which sank in 1912)*

Clearly, none of us is immune. The only thing we can do is be prepared.

THE BEST TIME TO SELL MIGHT BE TOMORROW

Given the benefits of selling when you want to, the shortened cycle of growth, and the possibility of adverse unexpected events, it stands to reason that business owners should always be ready to consider the possibility of a sale and always be prepared to welcome that unexpected knock on the door from a prospective acquirer who just has to have your business now (for a premium price, of course). A substantial percentage of portfolio companies owned by private equity groups are sold in just such a fashion—someone unexpectedly made them an offer they could not refuse and they opportunistically accepted (and were ready to do so). If a great opportunity arises, you need to be in a position to quickly take advantage of it. Like a home seller, you don't know when that perfect buyer is going to walk through the door. So, in essence, you need to make sure your house is always properly painted, the windowpanes are repaired, the furniture is correctly positioned, and you're ready for buyers to stop by.

Every business has its own life cycle, and at a critical juncture, when the numbers are good, you have to have your exit strategy in place. Suppose you had a wonderful opportunity to sell, you didn't, and then everything went to hell? Maybe the downturn had nothing to do with your managerial skills or the decision you made to not sell when you could have. Suppose you ended up losing your shirt, and after you moved from your wonderful twelve-room house to a four-room apartment, you told your spouse that you could have gotten out of the business a year ago. How would your spouse reply?

When business owners are approached by the right buyers, even when the owners aren't completely ready to sell, the opportunity might be too good to pass up. But the value you receive can depend heavily on your readiness. If your company is in a ready position for sale, it might be valued at $6 million. If it's not, it might be worth $3.5 million or $4 million, because the prospective buyer will have to deal with the issues that you have not addressed. For example, sometimes a business's potential value in preparation for sale is held back because business owners have never had audited financial statements. (Plus, if the business is not ready, a prospective buyer may not even want to pursue the sale.)

BETTER TO SELL TOO EARLY THAN TOO LATE

If you've been a small business owner at the helm of the venture you founded for ten to twenty years, or more, the realization might have snuck up upon you that when an opportune moment arrives to sell your business, you need to move more quickly than ever before. It's easy to get caught off guard.

Perhaps you modeled your business on what you learned from your father, another relative, or a mentor. You saw someone grow a business over many years or decades, and then sold for great value. It may seem logical to presume that such a scenario will define how things would go for you. But today, your golden opportunity might come within a few months or years, or tomorrow. You'll be caught flat-footed if you're operating under the old paradigm that you should build up a business for many years or decades, or a lifetime, before you sell.

As I said, in today's economy, everything is happening at a faster and faster pace. No one can afford to wait around for several years, because that gives competitors the opportunity to encroach upon a business's success. Still, many business owners will put up their feet and say, "Why should I sell now when I might do even better next year?"

You might do better next year, but you might not. For example, when an industry is consolidating, owners must be prepared to accept good offers when they come or be left behind to perish. A few years back, two companies, OMC and Yamaha, were buying companies in the boating industry left and right. One highly successful business owner in the industry decided not to accept the knock on the door from either of these potential buyers. Two things happened: first, the industry tanked, and second, no more buyers appeared. The owner's window of opportunity to achieve maximum returns for the sale of his business had closed.

It's far better to sell too early than to sell too late. Attempting to sell too late often equates to no possibility to sell at all. The intangible value of your business—mainly, the goodwill associated with the company—can evaporate when you attempt to sell too late in the game. Like a home in the real estate market that's been on the books for a long time, a business that has long been available for sale raises concerns of other potential buyers. What's wrong with this company? Why has it been on the market for so long? How come no one has grabbed it?

If you end up selling earlier than you wanted to or expected to, the saving grace is that you have the opportunity to do something else. If you succeeded in one business, you can succeed in another.

THE BENEFITS OF PARTNERING

One thing to keep in mind: selling need not mean exiting your business. You can sell some of your equity to a partner and keep a stake in your company. Noam Wasserman's *Harvard Business Review* study indicates that business owners who partner with others do better in the long run than those who go it alone. This might seem counterintuitive. After all, partnering with others means that you have to split the pie. But what if, as a result of partnering, the pie gets a lot bigger? The answer: more pie for you.

Entrepreneurs tend to be hard-driving types who play their cards close to the vest. They often have difficulty grappling with the notion of partnership. Yet, teaming up with the right partner often results in greater success than could otherwise be achieved. One of the important messages we convey to our clients is that partnering can be a personal and business decision with very positive outcomes. Repeatedly, we have seen that the best private middle-market owners/entrepreneurs, as well as the firms that invest in them, are able to achieve a synergistic effect as a result of unions with others.

In time, many founders acknowledge that their demonstrated ability to motivate others, unflagging enthusiasm, and financial resources are not quite sufficient for capitalizing on the opportunities that could vault their companies to a higher level. When grappling with such a reality, the entrepreneur may seek out venture capitalists, angel investors, or even the resources of friends and family members.

Business owners who are able to let go have opportunities to increase their wealth many times over what they could realize by going it alone. Historically, giving up a measure of control has resulted in substantial financial gain for the founder, not merely in terms of a percentage point increase in annual personal income, but as a **multiple** of the earnings. As Wasserman adroitly observes, "A founder who gives up more equity to attract investors builds a more valuable company than one who parts with less—and ends up with a more valuable slice, too." In other words, the founder who has the wherewithal to partner with others does exceedingly better financially than he would otherwise.

Here are some key reasons why:

Broadened perspective. Most business owners tend to be myopic. They know what they know, which may be limited, and they don't know what they don't know, which may be vast. Because they are often hard-driving, Type A personalities, they often lack the circle of friends or advisors that could help them maintain perspective and recognize new opportunities. But when a private equity group, or PEG, buys a company, for example, it always installs a knowledgeable board of directors. The owner who stays on board with an equity share of the company now has a sounding board unlike anything previously experienced. This newly assembled board of directors has a perspective and an inclination toward long-term planning that simply was not available to the owner prior to the acquisition.

13

First or forgotten. Entire industries have been dominated by firms that were first in the marketplace, even when their product or service idea wasn't as innovative as someone else's. The invention and development of rubber by Bessemer and by Firestone represent a prime example. Both developed their products at the same time, but Firestone was more effective in reaching the marketplace. Today, Firestone tires are still a standard in the industry, while the name Bessemer is all but forgotten. Ideas, like products and businesses, also have a shelf life, and their value is perishable. A game changer will not remain as such forever. Someone else will emerge with a rival or substitutable product or service. The idea might not quite be the same, but if another company is first to the marketplace, what they offer may be sufficient for enough customers, who didn't know what else was possible.

Entrepreneurs acting on their own without partners incur capital growth losses because of a failure to seize opportunities. PEGs know this, so when thinking about acquiring an owner's business, they ask a standard question: "If you had unlimited capital, what would you do?" The unwary business owner's response might often be the make-or-break factor in the PEG's decision to acquire the business.

We worked a client who was a legend in his own industry and a nationally known speaker to boot. His forte was developing new products. Many of the product prototypes sitting on his plant floor—some of them potential industry game changers—had never gone past the prototype stage. He was endlessly tied up in the claptrap of running the business and didn't want to invest the money required to fully develop his novel ideas. Failing to see the big picture of maximizing the value of his business, the priorities he focused on were second-tier compared with what he could accomplish. He didn't understand the true costs involved in *not* pursuing his game-changing ideas. PEGs, by contrast, are predisposed to monetize opportunities as they become aware of them. They know that a good idea not acted upon swiftly can be lost forever.

14

If the owner has several viable ideas, this stokes the imagination and enthusiasm of the PEG in many ways. PEG managers know that additional capital can fuel research that results in viable new product lines or can be used to invest in more efficient machinery, which dramatically reduces costs and can fuel business development efforts, because there are more "feet on the street."

Founding, running, and growing a business take different skills. Wasserman discusses what he calls "the founder's dilemma." He studied 212 domestic start-up companies founded in the late 1990s to the early 2000s. Most of these ventures' owners surrendered all or part of their managerial duties well before their respective companies went public. By the third anniversary of the business, only half of the founders held the position of CEO. By the fourth anniversary, the number was down to 40 percent. Less than one in four presided over their company's initial public offering. Other studies have observed the same phenomena in a variety of industries. The few founders or CEOs who have become household names are the exceptions, not the rule. On their way to extreme wealth, most founders who were able to grab the brass ring shifted from having complete control and ownership of the company to relinquishing both. Often, those who maintain rigid control of their companies achieve financial returns well below the business potential. Such founders are rich in ego rewards but little else.

Founders don't easily relinquish their reigns of power. In Wasserman's research, 90 percent were forced by investors to abandon their post as CEO. Four out of five founders strongly resisted giving up control, even when the board of directors found that the need for change was abundantly clear. They were hurt, shocked, and reluctant to step aside long before they ever intended to do so. They tended to believe that because they had already demonstrated competence, it just made sense for them to continue on in their leadership role. "I've brought the company this far," the founder reasons, "I can bring it to the next stage, too." The problem is that the journey from point A to point B often has little relationship with the journey from point B to point C. The founder must recognize that leaders in ventures of all sizes face new types of challenges that are unprecedented in the history of their companies.

The skills and attributes needed to found a company are often very different from those needed to grow a company. As soon as the first product is shipped or the first service delivered, the company switches from starting up to growing. The founder must now lead the company over the hurdles of selling greater volumes, increasing the customer base, providing service after the sale, managing inventory, maintaining and growing a competent and viable staff, managing the company's increasingly intricate finances, meeting new tax burdens, keeping pace with applicable regulations, and so on.

For most companies, the expanding needs of the business eventually outstrip the founder's ability to successfully remain at the helm. Paradoxically, the faster the founder was able to lead his or her company to the place at which enhanced management expertise and outside funding is essential, the more rapidly that founder will likely to have to relinquish management control if the company is to be a success. Said another way, "Success makes founders less qualified to lead the company and changes the power structure so they are more vulnerable."

And change is the rule, not the exception. Outside investors tend to have their greatest leverage just prior to their cash injection into the founder's company. Most often, investors use that leverage to mandate that the founder take his or her optimal role. Most PEGs, for example, require 50.1 percent or more ownership (i.e., control) following the investment/acquisition in any company in which they invest. However, **if a business is acquired by a PEG, the PEG will likely ask the owner to stay on and to retain equity.** This can be advantageous for all concerned. **Your company can grow on somebody else's dime, while you can sell a portion of your**

retained equity and realize far more than you would have had you sold the whole company. This might sound too good to be true, but I can give you one example after another.

Here's one: we sold a recycling business at a price between $10 million and $20 million. The owner kept 25 percent of the business, along with the rights to buy additional stock. The buyer continued to make acquisitions and to grow organically and strengthen the business. As the business grew, its valuation multiplied. The owner's 25 percent equity continues to rise. Management believes the 25 percent equity he retained will be worth $40 million within four years [no personal guarantees, no more invested capital out of pocket, and, having cashed in some chips, his family has a secure financial future.)

In terms of magnitude, that's an extraordinary return. It is not extraordinary, however, to have business owners retain a portion of their companies and then actually sell that portion later for a greater sum than the majority of the company sold for.

Remember the list of reasons why owners sell their businesses? Well, here's another: if you retain some ownership, it's a great way to diversify your assets. From a financial planning perspective, this diminishes your risk profile. As one of our mentors said, "Let's say I'm your financial advisor. If I recommended you invest 75 percent of your assets in one privately held, illiquid asset, you'd fire me immediately. But $6 million of your $8 million net worth is in your 100 percent-owned business." And that's exactly the situation that most business owners are in: **overexposed to a single asset, their own business.**

Another compelling reason to sell but retain equity is that you can grow the company without signing any personal guarantees. This is huge. Operating on OPM—other people's money—yields tremendous personal and professional advantages.

MAKING THE RIGHT DECISION FOR YOU

Even with the financial benefits available, we understand that not all business owners will be convinced to sell part or all of their businesses. It's not always about making a fortune. Many studies reveal that start-up business owners make only as much as they would have made as employees somewhere else. Considering the higher risk in launching a venture, their personal earnings often are not admirable. Something else is driving them: the need to be at the helm of their own enterprise and to be free to follow the dictates of their creativity and imagination, perhaps.

The founder who wishes to retain control hasn't necessarily made a poor choice, even though the odds are overwhelming that the business will never become as valuable monetarily as it otherwise could. Most vital is how well the founder's choice meshes with his or her objective for launching the venture in the first place. Some are aware that continuing to hold tightly to the reigns will prevent the company from achieving its optimal potential, but they can't let go because of personal and emotional factors.

If you cannot wholeheartedly embrace the requirements of a partnership, you should not undertake one. A founder who is too emotionally involved to maintain objectivity can become a liability to his own company. As a new, more viable board emerges, if the founder fights against accepting a lesser role, the ensuing struggle can cause wear and tear on a young venture. If loyal employees are opposed to the founder's "demotion," it can sometimes doom the venture entirely.

Yet most founders seek both control **and** wealth. As they begin to realize that they will need to surrender one to maximize the other, they experience a brief period of decision-making hibernation in which they weigh all of the alternatives. Wasserman found that entrepreneurs face a continual choice between managing their venture and generating their revenues. Neither aim is necessarily more worthy than the other, but **it is important to pick one**. The founder who doesn't make this decision too frequently gains neither power nor wealth. Those who are able to firmly embark on a course of action, be it holding back or bringing in the big guns, gain peace of mind. Wasserman concludes that founders who surrender total control can even find it mentally and emotionally attractive to be part of a changing management structure, because they are now going to benefit from other people's money and management skills. Those who focus on the wealth potential of the venture more easily surrender to a new CEO, and in many cases initiate the search themselves. As the company's finances become more involved, the founder must be dependent on skilled financial executives and veteran accountants. As the company grows and develops in structure, the founder becomes part of the managerial hierarchy, with specialized roles and formal procedures. Such founders/CEOs have a greater propensity to cooperate with their board of directors in establishing their own new roles and responsibilities following this planned succession. Founders who believe that their venture holds considerable potential for success are more likely to agree to surrender the reigns.

Founders who realize that their true objective is to amass significant wealth do not tend to suffer from identity crises. They don't consider themselves failures as they step aside from the company's top posts. Indeed, they are doing exactly what legions of other wealthy founders of startups have done: partner and win. In addition, the founder who is willing to surrender equity to lure PEGs, investors, and others to fulfill key management functions ends up bolstering the company in ways that would not happen otherwise.

MOTIVATION IS KEY

In our business, we as intermediaries help to prepare middle-market business owners for acquisition by PEGs or synergistic acquirers. One of the axioms is that if the business sale is to work, the business owner needs to be motivated. Motivation is the glue that holds everything together and makes the transaction work. Outside investors often determine whether to pursue investing in a company based on whether the founder is motivated by generating great wealth. If not, many will pass and take a look at the next business opportunity.

The reason that motivation is so crucial is that executing a successful transition is labor-intensive, time-consuming, costly, risky, and downright difficult to pull off. In most cases, business owners experience significant hurdles between the time when they first have the intent to sell and when the sale is actually consummated. See the Readiness Matrix, below. You are not truly ready to sell until you are the lower right space on the quadrant.

In virtually every case, understanding the results of achieving your goals from both the personal and financial perspectives are paramount to mustering the motivation that will see you through to the realization of that goal. Human beings, as creatures of habit, have a fear of the unknown and prefer to avoid risk. If you don't know what life is like on the other side, after you sell the business, you're going to stay with what you know. The more you know about what's on the other side, the real benefits, and the opportunities that can emerge, the better you're going to be at preparing your business for acquisition. We work to provide business

Readiness Matrix

Business not ready Owner no mindset to sell	Business is ready Owner no mindset to sell
Business not ready Owner has mindset to sell	Business is ready Owner has mindset to sell

Adapted from
Exiting Your Business, Protecting Your Wealth by John Leonetti

owners with a realistic portrayal of the potential of selling their businesses.

As a business owner myself for the past twenty-six years, I've developed a deep sense of appreciation for our clients. All the professionals in my company want our clients to do well. We want our clients to feel good about the acquisition terms of the deals before they make them, and we want them to reap the rewards for all the years of sacrifice and hard work that they've devoted to their businesses.

The best way to do this is to take a look at the practices of PEGs, which I've mentioned throughout this chapter. They are the experts at creating maximum wealth in purchasing, growing, and selling businesses. In the next chapter, we'll take a closer look at what exactly PEGs are and what they do.

Chapter 2: Private Equity 101

So far in this book, I've thrown the term PEG around a great deal. As a business owner, you've probably heard about private equity groups, but you may not fully understand what they are and what they do. This chapter provides a little background.

Private Equity and Venture Capital: Not the Same Thing

To understand the role and mission of PEGs, let's first differentiate between private equity groups and venture capitalists. PEGs invest in established, middle-market companies, whereas venture capital firms invest in startups. A world of difference exists between the two.

You hear more about venture capital firms than you do about PEGs. Venture capitalists are the subjects of magazines and newspaper articles, and they draw attention when they hit grand slams. For example, the venture capitalists who invested in Google, Apple, and Microsoft when they were young gained considerable fame and notoriety once the companies began to do well.

PEGs enjoy a quieter form of success. **PEGs aggregate funds from high-net-worth individuals, insurance companies, institutions, and other groups that have pooled funds and use them to acquire**

businesses that show promise. PEGs represent a systematic, disciplined way of investing in smaller, privately owned companies with high potential for growth—organic or through additional acquisitions, or both—leading to opportunities for multiplying the group's initial equity investment.

With their rigorous screening processes for deciding in which businesses to invest, their financial analysis, their database of subject-matter experts, and the systematic way in which they help maximize businesses' value, PEGs provide a valuable service to investors, large and small, who don't have the time, energy, or capability to undertake such analysis. Investors benefit from the diversification that the PEGs provide, as well as their expertise in making, growing, and selling acquisitions. If I'm a high-net-worth individual seeking to invest in an up-and-coming company, it's well within my interests to work with a group that engages in this kind of acquisition all the time. It's a tough world out there with a lot of risk, so when I find a group that has done a lot of the spade work in evaluating which companies represent good investments, that group has got my attention.

There are two basic types of PEGs: dedicated funds and pledge funds.

- **Dedicated funds.** A dedicated fund has a pool of capital pledged to it by its investors specifically for the purpose of making acquisitions. Suppose a PEG has $100 million pool of capital to invest. When the group makes all the acquisitions it can with that particular fund, it will seek to raise another fund, perhaps of $200 million, for more acquisitions. It receives funding from many sources, including high-net-worth individuals, insurance companies, endowment funds, universities, banks, and even sovereign governments that choose to invest in private equity firms, such as China.

- **Pledge funds.** With a pledge fund, the PEG identifies a target company for acquisition then appeals to its list of investors to raise the capital to make that acquisition. There is more risk in raising pledge funds because each investment stands on its own; thus the investors are not diversified within the fund.

Many small business owners start with nothing. They have a talent for producing some type of product or service. The typical business owner continually reinvests in the company, but that reinvestment is in the form of sweat equity: time, effort, and labor. One entrepreneur I encountered who was in the construction business had pretax earnings of $2.5 million. I asked him what his equity investment in the company was, and he said, "Zero." I asked, "Do you know the return on that?" He correctly replied, "Infinite."

> For more information about PEGs, contact the Private Equity Growth Capital Council. The Council, based in Washington, DC, was established in 2007 and serves as an advocacy, communications, research, and resource center that "develops, analyzes and distributes information about the private equity and growth capital investment industry and its contributions to the national and global economy." PEGCC members represent "the best-known and most-respected" PEGs. Visit www.pegcc. org for a wealth of industry data and background.

The investment a PEG makes once acquiring such a company is of a totally different nature. The comparison is apples and oranges. The typical PEG seeks the larger variety of middle-market businesses, generally those that are more mature and have been built up over many years. The PEG is predisposed to invest in its acquisitions, often leveraging debt to acquire equipment or expand facilities. Without these investments—that is, continuing on the path forged by the company's founder—the company's probable value at the time of sale would only be a fraction of its value after having been acquired by a PEG.

The PEG may grow the company internally, rationalize its operations, or make complimentary acquisitions—either horizontal (other businesses in the same industry) or vertical (other companies involved in making or selling the product). In doing so, it increases the company's value substantially prior to executing a well-thought-out exit or sale (through a sale to a synergistic acquirer or a larger private equity group, or via taking it public).

The typical PEG manager is someone who began as an associate or financial analyst with another PEG. Prior to working for any PEG, he or she might also have been in financial management of some sort. In other words, managers have not necessarily been entrepreneurs themselves. At a certain point in their careers, these associates or financial analysts have accumulated enough experience to make the decision to start their own funds. Often, they will partner with others who have risen through the ranks with them. Many PEG managers have MBAs.

Financial analysts in PEGs are responsible for deciding which companies to consider among many available for acquisition. PEGs do not, however, typically directly manage the companies that they acquire. (That's why they often want the owner to stay on board and manage the enterprise after the closing.)

PEGs and the Middle Market

Middle-market businesses range in value from $1 million to $150 million, a large spread. Above $150 million is Wall Street territory, not Main Street territory. At this level, multi-billion-dollar PEGs such as Goldman Sachs, J.P. Morgan, and other mergers and acquisitions firms dominate. Below about $150 million, the smaller, lesser known, middle-market PEGs predominate.

How PEGs get paid. In a PEG's contract with its investors, the investors are slated to receive back 100 percent of their money

26

before the PEG receives its fee (a "carried interest") for participation in the sale of the acquired business. PEGs also typically receive a management fee from each portfolio company and sometimes a small percentage of the total amount of funding under management. The annual management fee paid by an acquired company during the time the PEG owns and manages it could range from $125,000 to $300,000. Some PEGs also receive a fee when they make an acquisition. Our view is that the better PEGs do not engage in this latter practice.

Many PEG managers co-invest in their own funds. This shows great confidence in their abilities to make their passive investors a very healthy rate of return. Some PEGs also increase returns with a strategy employing preferred debt or equity, or both. Once again, the PEG managers receive 20 percent of that preferred return after the investors have received 100 percent of their original investment. While a few PEGs receive a fee associated with the acquisition of a company, some also receive a fee when the acquired company is finally sold.

Imagine that a PEG spends $1 million to acquire majority equity in a company. Five years later, after paying off all debt and all fees, that equity investment grows to $5 million. The PEG receives 20 percent of the increase over the original equity investment. So, of the $4 million equity increase, the PEG would receive $800,000. That $800,000 represents the PEG's participation for originating the transaction, managing the business, and selling that investment out of the fund. The remaining $3.2 million goes to the investors, in addition to the investors' original $1 million. This is 4.2 times their original investment. As the typical holding period runs three to seven years, this represents quite a lucrative return.

(During the time a PEG owns a company or a group of companies, investors don't anticipate receiving distributions. They want earnings to be reinvested to maximize growth. The faster the value of a company rises, the greater the chance its annual revenues will rise as well.)

Multiplying value. Going further, if a company is acquired for $1 million in earnings before interest, taxes, depreciation, and amortization (EBITDA, see Chapter 5) and sells for a *five-multiple*, the company's worth is $5 million. The $4 million rise in EBITDA is the result of increases in earnings, the paying down of debt, the achievement of critical mass as a result of in-depth management, and a more diverse customer and supplier base, to name a few. Because of these improvements, there is less risk associated with the continuity of income. Hence, the company could now command a seven-multiple instead of a five-multiple in a sale to the next acquirer. The PEG's involvement has increased the value of the company. If what predictably could have sold at a five-multiple now has the potential for a seven-multiple, then investors can gain a substantial return on their original invested capital.

Let's talk about debt. The companies sought by PEGs generally have tremendous growth potential and perhaps are high visibility targets of and for investors. In such ventures, the founders, business owners, or managers often reach a point when they are leery of borrowing any money or signing any personal guarantees. Herein lies a paradox. By refusing to reinvest in their companies, these owners often end up stifling growth. PEGs know that debt, when used wisely, can enhance a company's growth and profitability. As long as the returns continue to accrue, PEGs will invest and invest again. It makes good sense. The 20 percent carried interest that PEGs make when they resell a business can be huge if the business sells for a high multiple.

The offering memorandum. When PEGs are ready to sell their acquisitions, or owners are ready to sell their businesses, they prepare an offering memorandum. The memorandum offers a narrative about the company, a recap of its finances, and a projection as to its future performance. It includes such basic information as a description of the founding of the company and the background of the owners, the facilities, the products and services, the pricing, and the known competitors. An offering memorandum may go by other names, such as a confidential business review or a confidential marketing memorandum, but in each instance, the document serves the same purpose.

When a PEG is ready to sell a portfolio company, it follows a specific set of steps. Even if the PEG has owned a company for five years and that company still has significant growth opportunities, if it's time for the private equity group to reap its rewards, it will: the company has reached a sufficient critical mass to be of interest to larger PEGs or other buyers.

The dirty little secret. Most businesses, whether they work with an intermediary or not, do not sell, at least not the first time they try. (This unfortunate reality is something you're not likely to hear from others within my industry.) This may be because the business isn't ready, is not valuable to potential acquirers, or lacks the proper business positioning to attract investors.

Conversely, PEGs are able to sell nearly 100 percent of the companies they acquire. **What do PEGs know that business owners do not? Plenty.** What if you could learn the secrets of PEGs so that you could be among that handful of richly rewarded entrepreneurs who sell their businesses at maximum value? By learning to generate wealth the ways PEGs do, you'll understand, in brief, how to notably improve your company in ways that could result in a much higher valuation. In the next chapter, I'll lay out the strategies and tactics PEGs use to maximize company value.

INTERVIEW: QUESTIONS AND ANSWERS WITH VETERAN PEG MANAGER

Here is an insider's look at the thinking and operations of a PEG manager. Jason (name disguised) has been a partner in a PEG for twenty-four years and has been a principal in one hundred twenty-six acquisitions in fifty-one industries. His insights are illuminating.

Bob: What's your range for acquiring a business?

Jason: Between $2 to $7 million of EBITDA (pretax, pre-interest, pre-depreciation/amortization earnings), the lower-middle market in private equity.

Bob: What attributes make you want to acquire a company?

Jason: We look at debt leverage, stability of cash flow, and growth potential. We look to partner with companies we acquire. We seek strong management, whether it's incumbent or whether we recruit for the company. We avoid companies competing in a commodity-oriented sector; this typically means we're investing in companies with a healthy EBITDA. For manufacturing or distributors, we're looking for 10 percent or higher. We're not interested in average margins of 5 percent. The companies we seek have higher barriers to entry. They are doing something that not everyone can do.

Bob: What else makes a company appealing to you?

Jason: Sales that are not hyper-cyclical, companies not prone to technological obsolescence, companies in industries not prone to fashion or fad orientation, and companies not prone to legislative challenges. We stay away from companies prone to interruption of the stability of the performance.

30

Bob: How many companies do you look at before you make a single acquisition?

Jason: Last year, we considered 1,700 deals. In a solid year, we'll acquire three. We are grateful for people who err on the side of inclusion and show us any deals that could conceivably be of interest. We encourage wide interpretation of candidate companies, because we want to make our own assessment. Most of what we encounter is not appropriate because of size or industry. We provide quick, courteous, and detailed feedback to our deal sources, knowing that most submissions will be rejected.

Bob: If a business meets your initial criteria, what defects prompt you to reject it?

Jason: The finances. Often, you'll see bad financial results in a strong industry. If we sense that the owners or operators are not honorable people, we'll walk away. If the company is having unique legal challenges, thorny environmental problems, or any kind of pending negative issue, we'll withdraw. If the company has no such problems, but the owner has unreasonable pricing expectations, it's often too much of a hurdle.

Bob: Once you own a company, how do you enhance its value?

Jason: Our firm has a strong internal operations capability. We have partners who were themselves serial CEOs, COOs, and CFOs, who give us the bandwidth to shoulder projects or engage in operational improvements. We build value by increasing the profitability of the company and by strengthening the management team, if necessary. By cleaning up the finances and the financial systems, and by bringing rigor to the accounting, the company will have a more sophisticated management information system and thus will generate the vital information.

Broadly, we professionalize and optimize all functional areas of the business. A company could be highly profitable, but doesn't 'show well' physically. A bit of window dressing could make it more acceptable to the next buyer. We also seek to eliminate distractions from main business that don't contribute to profitability. This can be important operationally in helping to attract the eventual suitor.

Bob: For overall returns, do you favor add-on acquisitions or organic growth?

Jason: It depends on the industry and company. We've been fortunate to have portfolio companies grow tenfold or more, both by organic growth and by key acquisitions. Sometimes, it's a combination of the two.

Bob: Do you employ an acquisition checklist and say, "Here's an opportunity for improvement?"

Jason: When our group of partners assesses an opportunity, we absolutely focus on the salient issues: the positives, or the growth opportunities, and the negatives, or the challenges facing the business. There is a mental checklist. We highlight the positives and the negatives, and we make an assessment.

Bob: What offensive strategies, such as fostering tremendous growth or making a key acquisition, and what defensive strategies, such as building a moat around the company's assets and reputation, do you follow?

Jason: We make sure the company has plenty of flexibility and the liquidity necessary for stability and growth. Defensively speaking, it's vital to have enough for both. Defensively and offensively: ensuring that the management team is solid. If the company is growing, but the team is not sufficient to manage that growth, it can be disastrous. We have to ensure we have the human assets to manage growth.

Having real-time accounting and financial information helps us foresee problems on the horizon, identify the root causes, and find applicable remedies. That's important. Having a better understanding of the company and more advance warning of any challenges is more important than when the company was entrepreneurial. Sometimes playing defense involves protecting patents or intellectual property, which is expensive and difficult, but must be handled.

Bob: What about competition?

Jason: You have to size up the competition. Before we acquire a firm, we do intensive market studies. These involve gathering intelligence from customers and the competitors themselves to clarify the competitive advantages and disadvantages we would have. Defensively and offensively, we seek a better understanding of the competitive strengths and weaknesses and what can be done about them.

Bob: Many business owners won't modify their pricing for fear of alienating long-time customers. What's your attitude toward pricing?

Jason: It's a fine balance. We encounter entrepreneurs who've never tested their pricing umbrella and are leaving sales volume and profits on the table. In those cases, we support a more sophisticated approach to pricing, but one can be too aggressive. It's important to understand the competitive landscape and not move too quickly, but we do believe in optimizing the pricing.

Bob: What percentages of your companies sell from a knock on the door that was unsolicited, as opposed to your planned exit?

Jason: We've had potential suitors proactively knock on our door. When they are strategic buyers, we've been more successful in quietly negotiating a transaction. Otherwise, we market our companies to both strategic and financial buyers. Roughly half of our sales have been to strategic buyers and half to larger financial buyers.

Bob: What determines it's time to sell a portfolio company?

Jason: We engage with our partners and are influenced by the desires of the people running the company. Typically, former owners are still on board, and we consider their goals and what they want to achieve. We look at the industry as a whole to assess any solid growth opportunities or new risks. Then, we make a judgment call as to whether or not the potential incremental gains justify any incremental risks.

Bob: In preparing to sell, what steps help you maximize the selling value?

Jason: The major step during our tenure is to bring in the operating assistance we need to make the company an attractive target in the first place. Having long groomed the company for our ultimate exit, we typically engage an investment bank to conduct a thorough exam of what's needed.

Bob: Other than hiring an investment-banking firm, what else would you do six to twelve months before you decide to make an offer on the company?

Jason: The list is long. Many entrepreneurs, particularly as they get into their later years, are not eager to make incremental investments, even when those investments have a fast payback. We invest continually when it strengthens the business; it's not as scary to us. We know how and when to do it, and we're happy to pursue opportunities. Beyond improving the accounting information and marketing information, we increase the efficiency of processes.

We convert manufacturers to cellular manufacturing techniques, if that's appropriate. We root out waste or inefficiency, roll up our sleeves, and improve efficiency and productivity. We serve as coaches, if needed. We believe that everybody wants to do well in their jobs, so we invest in the tools and equipment that people need to be effective.

We measure performance in specific functional areas, because you can't improve what you can't measure. We help recruit people to fill in roles, whether it's a company's first CFO, first head of logistics, or first true director of sales and marketing. We help build sales and marketing organizations, as well as supporting information systems, both domestically and abroad.

Bob: Why would an entrepreneur want to partner with a PEG?

Jason: Partnering with the right party is vital. If an owner partners with someone who is willing to over-lever the business, risk has escalated. Or, if they partner with people who have not helped other companies make the right decisions, then partnering is not going to reduce risk or increase the value of the business.

Bob: Assume a company is on your radar screen and they meet your criteria. Why should they partner with you? Why would they be better off than going it alone?

Jason: The entrepreneurs that we partner with are excellent at what they do. However, it's rare for anyone to be good at everything. Many entrepreneurs have areas of great strength and some blind spots, possibly in finance, sales, or marketing. They might be strong in product development and understand the market, but they might be missing out somewhere else.

For an entrepreneur who owns and runs a company of that size, to be perfectly well rounded and not have any blind spots is barely possible. We can make the company stronger and better and help it to grow and increase in capacity. We can help manage that growth, providing remedies in functional areas that are not strong. Weakness can be a limiting factor and contribute to risk, so we optimize the functional areas of the company and eliminate weak spots.

Having a capital partner is also vital. We've helped companies through unforeseen circumstances, including one company that was hit hard by Hurricane Katrina. It's pretty difficult to plan for that, right? Having an equity partner who injects money into the company and provides assistance in critical times is a strong defense.

Obviously, having the capital supports taking advantage of good growth opportunities.

Bob: It's tough to find the right party at the right price to handle the situation the first time around.

Jason: Right. By the time a business owner partners with us, they've gotten to know our history, our accomplishments, and us. If someone hires a consultant that they haven't known for long, it is a different proposition from a quality, batting average, and security standpoint than tasking a known-quantity partner that you've thoroughly vetted.

Many entrepreneurs like to have the "right" private equity partner, because it can be lonely at the top. Some entrepreneurs do not distribute information and do not delegate responsibilities broadly throughout the organization. They seek others with a lot of experience so that they can bounce around ideas together.

Bob: Yes. The expected lifetime of any particular business is shortening, and the competition can be extreme. Partnering with someone who has high-level expertise both diminishes risk on the defensive side and helps the company take advantage of potentially lost opportunities on the offensive side.

Jason: I agree. If your competitor can quickly become stronger and more sophisticated, then it behooves you to maximize your strengths, efficiencies, and level of sophistication.

Bob: In many industries, is it winner-take-all? Customers are often attracted to the best.

Jason: We've had portfolio companies that benefitted when large competitors fell on hard times. These competitors were not strongly positioned, and they did not have the resources that we provide. They faltered, and we were the benefactors.

Bob: Suppose you were teaching a class of entrepreneurs, and they are half the size necessary to be eligible for acquisition. What should they do to become eligible?

Jason: We are willing to work with companies that haven't undergone the improvements we would bring to them. If companies are too small, the challenge will be to grow revenues or add an acquisition, which would make the overall investment sufficiently large in size.

Sometimes, identifying strategically attractive and appropriate acquisitions can make the difference. You have to be mindful of the complexity. I've certainly looked at a company and thought, "It's too small, but if we made an add-on or two, that could make the difference." So, you have to find acquisitions that will become large enough.

Bob: When you look at the after-tax net to the owner who partners with a PEG, the owner earns more upon the PEG's sale to the next buyer than he made when he was in full ownership of the company.

Jason: We certainly have that good fortune, yes.

Bob: Why own a company if you're not going to produce great financial results? It's like owning a racecar and not caring about how fast it goes. It's fine to get into a business where you excel and build a great company, but at a certain point, maturation requires strategic direction. The reason you do such a good job managing companies is that you know the goal when you start out: you know exactly what you want to accomplish. If you didn't, you couldn't attract the investors that you have.

Jason: Exactly. Plenty of company owners don't relish the complexity beyond a certain level of growth. Some folks want to pass the company on to their children. In those cases, if the children are truly ready to take over the family business, that's fine.

It's best when people are self-aware, know their goals, and can determine the best path to meet those goals. If their goals include liquidity, diversification of net worth, and optimizing the growth of the business, and if they can find the *right* partner, it can be a highly positive experience.

The majority of times, people who partner with us can have their cake and eat it too. They achieve that liquidity and diversification, and they continue to run the company that they've built. They don't have to do it alone, and they retain a degree of ownership. The value of their minority retained equity stake may well be worth more upon a subsequent sale (by the original owner and the PEG) than the value of the initial majority interest – it happens quite frequently.)

It is important to have partners that you like and trust. Hopefully, owners will partner with a fund where the people will act like partners, think about the owner-operators, and structure the transaction so that something good happens for the owner-operator. They are attached at the hip and moving forward together, seeking to accomplish the same objectives. That's how good partnerships are built—when people are truly coming at it with a partnering mentality. They do what's prudent and make good judgments together.

Chapter 3: Maximizing Value the PEG Way

Throughout this book so far, I've implied that PEGs have a lot to teach middle-market business owners about how companies may be managed to maximize their value. In this chapter, I'll go further and discuss exactly what PEGs do to increase the value of the companies they buy. This information is not just to help you understand the benefit of possibly selling your company to a PEG—it's information you might want to consider incorporating into your management strategy today.

Why employ the practices and procedures of PEGs in the quest to sell your business for its maximum value? The answer: **PEGs consistently achieve 25 percent to 75 percent annual compounded rates of return on their equity investments, and they do it with acquisition after acquisition. That means a doubling, tripling, or quadrupling of their equity investments in a two- to five-year period.** (Using the "rule of 72," 25 percent annual returns equate to a doubling of the value of the company in three years.) Most notably, they often do it with less risk than is otherwise incurred by businesses in that market. How so? They have far greater knowledge than private business owners about a wide variety of inputs effecting value. In this case, knowledge absolutely is power.

41

Increasing the value of your business is vital, regardless of how long you intend to own it. Whether or not you are even entertaining the notion of selling the company, PEG-employed tactics and strategies represent lessons from which all business owners can draw to raise the value of their enterprises. The lessons that PEG managers have to offer will improve your business—irrefutably.

Some suggestions that I will provide might seem obvious. Others might be more subtle or might even be new information to you. Regardless, if you are not consistently undertaking value-enhancing steps in a coherent and vigorous manner, you can't come anywhere near to achieving the dramatic increase in equity that is within your grasp.

What Makes a PEG Look Twice

Whether you are making bread or making money, you have to start with good dough. The better managed a company already is, the more likely we, as intermediaries, will be able to both maximize the value of the company and sell it for the owner. PEGs are able to work with such companies and convert this "raw material" to something that is far more valuable, sometimes many times more valuable than when they acquired it. Often—and as incredible as it may sound—this value increase can occur with no greater assets, plants, or equipment. But first, they have to start with a business they know they can improve and sell.

Potential is essential. Simply put, PEGs look for companies with significant growth potential and realizable opportunities. When PEGs acquire a business, they explore growth potential in all avenues and develop a plan that harnesses the energies of you and your key staff to accelerate growth (in the top line and the bottom line.) If you are one of the top players in your industry, region, or local market, your company's potential for growth is vast. If you're merely a respectable player, the level of under-performance that you are experiencing in marketing, sales, finance, distribution, and so on nevertheless heralds ripe potential for growth. Suppose a specific type of business does well regionally, but the business owner does not have the management talent, capital, and skills to expand. PEGs and other savvy investors would easily spot the potential here. Typically, PEGs acquire a platform company—a company sufficiently large to support the infrastructure and the fees associated with the PEG's efforts. Thereafter, the PEG might seek similar companies to add onto the platform company. So, the platform company grows both organically, or internally, and through acquisitions, or externally.

Sometimes, an owner will approach a PEG, rather than the other way around. This most often happens when the PEG already owns a company or portfolio of companies in the same industry as the owner's. The PEG will not make a decision to buy such a company hastily. If it does so, however, this is called an add-on acquisition.

Since PEG managers earn their keep by making acquisitions, they have a high incentive to be on their game all the time. They won't, however, make acquisitions simply for the sake of making them and will not knowingly thwart their ability to earn an aggregate 25 percent to 50 percent compounded rate of return on their investments. Note: they may not make 25 percent on every investment. PEGs are measured on the totality of their success, not on any one particular deal.

Acquiring with an endpoint in mind. From the day a PEG acquires a business, it works to prepare that company for resale and strives to maintain the company in a ready state. Making a wise acquisition investment in the first place and improving its operations and financial performance are paramount to selling the acquisition effectively on the other end. Starting from ground zero, facing a blank page, PEGs work from the endpoint—the time at which they'll sell the business for a high value—back to the present. They ask penetrating questions, such as, "Why will someone want to acquire this company and/or its divisions? What will be the key deciding factors?" From there, they consider such questions as, "What can this company achieve? What can it become? What are the crucial initiatives that will offer the biggest payoff in three to five years?"

KEY STRATEGIES PEGs USE TO ENHANCE VALUE

Once a PEG has acquired a company, it follows a rigorous, time-tested process of identifying and capturing opportunities for growth, top line and bottom line (EBITDA.) The PEG's added value comes from its expertise, its ability to draw on outside talent, and its strict adherence to best management practices

Action plan. To exploit a company's full potential, PEG managers establish an action plan focusing on the handful of opportunity areas that hold the best potential for maximizing the company's value. PEGs determine who will be involved, what will be needed, when and where the action will take place, and how results will be achieved.

Plans set in motion are broken down to the operational level with individual assignments, timelines, milestones, and a finish line, in a project management-like fashion. A small business owner might only have the time and energy to launch one or two project campaigns, whereas a PEG can launch many at once, thus accelerating momentum. Rather than focusing on too short a time horizon, such as the next twelve months, or too long a time horizon, such as five to ten years, **most PEGs stay focused on a three- to five-year time frame for bringing a company to its optimal potential**.

Throughout the process of acquiring, improving, and selling a company, PEGs draw on the great advantage of a bursting Rolodex. One of a PEG manager's key responsibilities is to build a deep database of subject matter experts and industry contacts. The ability to call on specialists in law, real estate, marketing, sales, manufacturing, etc., saves time and money and enhances results. The ability to contact potential synergistic buyers and others in a variety of industries does the same.

Competitive analysis. Sizing up the competition is no easy feat. First, PEGs strive to understand how the acquired company's products and services match up against those of the top competitors. Questions PEGs ask include:

- Are upgrades needed?

- Do competitors have a notable advantage over us as a result of the product, service, feature, or benefits that only they offer?

- If we do nothing differently, how will that impact our relations with customers and the revenue we derive?

- If we upgrade our product line, what is our revenue market share potential? What are the associated risks?

- How does our pricing structure stack up against others?

- Is the cost of producing and delivering our goods competitive? If we're at a disadvantage, what operational efficiencies can we employ?"

- What can we do to compete if we're trailing the industry leaders?

- How can we leapfrog the competition to attain the lead?

- What coming changes in technology, regulation, and the business and social environment will impact what we do?

45

Understandably, determining the answers to these questions is no small task. Because PEGs work in teams, rely on subject matter experts, and inject dynamic energy into a company, they have the means to derive accurate and appropriate answers. They are not afraid to spend serious dollars to have an outside marketing research company find out exactly what they need to know. Ignorance is expensive. Key information is invaluable.

The surest path to selling for a high multiple is to increase a company's earnings while decreasing its associated risks. The next buyer wants to acquire a clean, financially well-managed entity. Since **PEGs maintain a seller's mentality from day one**, they examine every aspect of a business from a seller's perspective. Achieving operational efficiency and reducing expenses is a time-honored approach to maximizing value, as is having the right equipment, procedures, and people in place.

A universal truth about business owners is that they're weak in marketing, sales, and business development, even when they believe these to be their strengths. This weakness does not stem from their inability or reluctance to pound the pavement, dispatch a qualified sales force, or make things happen. It occurs as a result of not investing adequate funds in marketing and of failing to maintain the proper focus.

PEGs ponder the question, "What is this business capable of with an injection of more capital?" (Often, the owner knows the answer, and it represents a range of untapped opportunities. As such, the owner holds the key to the company's future capital growth and increase in value, and selling to a PEG can make it happen.)

Creating value might come from one or more bedrock strategies, such as:

Using debt with an eye to long-term gain. Many business owners are averse to debt. But PEGs know how to leverage debt for optimal gain, understanding that acquiring additional assets such as equipment or even a new plant may pay off big in the long run. All businesses need cash on hand for operating expenses, key acquisitions, and emerging opportunities. On his own, a middle-market business owner is unlikely to have as much cash on hand as a business acquired by a PEG. Keep in mind, however, that a business that incurs a high debt-to-equity ratio requires vigilant management to ensure that cash is dispensed judicially. Even in this economically challenged environment, good PEGs have maintained excellent lender relationships and can quite readily access/borrow the funds necessary for working capital and capital improvements (and they want to do so; they are driven to do so).

Diversifying customers and suppliers. Some entrepreneurs are overly invested in one key customer or a handful of customers (we call this *volume concentration*), missing other prime prospects in the niche. Some owners are too vested in patronizing a key supplier or a handful of key suppliers, missing out on the dramatic cost savings that could result from working with other vendors. If you manage your business with an eye to the sale, however, you would realize that a buyer would require a more diversified customer and supplier roster.

Streamlining operations. If PEGs acquire, say, a manufacturing company, opportunities abound for significantly improving efficiency. Currently, a movement is afoot among manufacturers everywhere, and particularly in the US, to operate based on **manufacturing cells**, whereby machines are grouped according to the parts or products they produce. Such an approach might be beyond the current capability of the owner. If so, the acquiring PEG will bring in an expert to redesign the shop floor, streamline the manufacturing process, and achieve operating efficiencies. If necessary, the PEG will invest in specific equipment to achieve desired operating efficiencies. Likewise, department by department, area by area, PEGs will determine what will contribute to the company's swiftest path to higher revenues, greater profitability, and maximum value.

Other strategies. These include extending channels of distribution, updating or broadening the product or service line, enhancing customer relations, and many others.

Many people hold the misconception that PEGs come in and eviscerate the company, much as some Wall Street firms do. That is far from the truth. Typically, PEGs are not keen on reducing staff in the newly acquired company. That sends the wrong message. The PEG's objective is to grow the company and become more efficient with the existing staff. PEGs invest in companies because of the people in those companies. Where the opportunities are apparent, they will enhance and bolster a company's human resources. That is where the PEG's extensive contact database comes into play. Example: Where a new sales manager may be advisable, the PEG will help management find, interview, hire, and manage that new sales manager.

Studies show that small businesses acquired by PEGs have an enhanced level of job creation compared to other businesses in the same industry and businesses throughout the larger economy. Likewise, PEG-managed enterprises generate greater value for shareholders while also offering achievement-oriented employees within a company the chance for greater opportunities, career growth, and increased earnings.

Don't be confused by the attention-grabbing headlines about investors/managers who sell off a company's assets or imprudently overload it with debt. The media often highlight random or rare occurrences, while missing the bigger, broader picture of what's really happening on Main Street.

THE PEG TEAM: ASSEMBLING THE RIGHT PEOPLE IN THE RIGHT PLACES

Any viable small business needs to have solid management and top talent in place. If already on board, this talent will be harnessed effectively to accomplish goals. If outside help is needed, PEGs seek to identify, attract, recruit, and retain specific talent. Entrepreneurial firms have less bureaucracy than much larger ones. PEGs often lure high-performance individuals through attractive compensation plans that are competitively and rationally crafted. We've witnessed many instances in which employees have been overpaid. PEGs retain compensation experts so they know they are competitive and properly compensating key performers.

A challenging environment can be stimulating to top achievers. Action-oriented managers and employees who buy into company objectives and proceed with an "owner's mentality" further help to accelerate progress towards desired results.

In addition, PEGs are skilled at attracting top talent for the company's board of directors. The new board's collective wisdom and experience helps to propel the company in ways that simply weren't possible prior to the sale.

THE PEG CULTURE

In addition to experience, contacts, and funding, the PEG attitude and culture go far toward enhancing company value.

Repeatable processes. When PEGs acquire a company, they seek to establish sustainable, effective processes that, once in place, contribute to increased long-term value. Immediately after a PEG acquires a business, before the ink on the sale agreement has dried, PEG managers shift into high gear. Following their own proprietary and established set of procedures, they work with the founder and other members of top management to identify, categorize, and act upon operational and strategic opportunities to increase profits.

In the first twelve months following acquisition, as a result of multiple initiatives and campaigns, PEGs can enjoy a return on investment (ROI) that is two to three times the industry norm. They do so by engaging in proven processes that can be repeated from company to company and within the company from department to department.

In particular, PEGs strive to achieve an in-depth understanding of the business's revenue and value potential by examining such critical areas as:

- Customer needs, wants, desires, goals, and objectives.

- The fundamental drivers of market demand, how it's changing, and what impact that will have on the industry in general and on the business in particular.

- The technological, environmental, regulatory, and social factors that could have an impact, positive or negative, on the company's performance.

- Direct competitors, indirect competitors, and, potentially, competitors from around the globe.

- The path of least resistance for the business to generate revenue: picking the low-hanging fruit by exploiting the most easily reached lucrative niches within the marketplace.

After acquiring such insights and assembling the data, PEGs typically adopt a three- to five-year time horizon through the preparation of a strategic plan for achieving their equity goal for the acquired company. The target is usually optimistic, if not exceedingly challenging. Yet, by proceeding along a new path, partnering with subject matter experts, executing strategies at an unprecedented pace within the business itself, and remaining focused, PEGs are confident that they can enable the business to grow in brand new ways.

Curiously, PEG managers maintain a rather modest disposition when evaluating a company for acquisition and in managing it after they've acquired it. They purposely do not assume a position of omnipotence. They recognize at the outset that they do not have complete and perfect knowledge of the business or industry. This is one reason why they seek to retain the company's founder and key employees when making an acquisition.

They also recognize that situations change more rapidly than ever before. The potential of a business three or six months ago does not equal its potential today or three or six months hence. So, once they've been handed management the reigns, they focus on the handful of crucial issues and initiatives that have the highest potential for propelling the business forward.

PEGs also clearly define what they are not prepared to do when managing the company. This enables them to maintain effectiveness, since no time is lost on paths predetermined to be outside the company's strategic focus.

Focus on measurable, critical data. PEG managers are numbers people. Their operating plans and key tactics are quantitatively measured to determine whether they are moving toward achievement. Key staff and vital resources are allocated accordingly. Market data and operational performance measures are used to keep the initiative on track.

PEG managers strive to maintain a keen focus on critical data to assure that the company continues to move in the desired direction. Internally, the culture begins the change. New jargon and new slogans reinforce employee efforts. Bonuses and other incentives ensure that desired performances are rewarded and repeated.

The accelerated momentum that PEGs can achieve within their acquired businesses often results in enhanced company performance. This sometimes occurs so rapidly that the momentum can build on itself.

A culture of achievement. From the first day of ownership, and often even before that, PEG managers foster a can-do attitude within the small businesses they acquire. This attitude is perhaps the most important thing PEGs bring to acquisitions. Levels of excitement build as the employees and staff begin to adopt a stronger focus on maximizing revenues and profitability.

Success in one area of the business can have a rippling effect on other areas. As opposed to putting out fires as they occur, PEG owners aggressively seek new methods and approaches to achieving challenging goals. Worn-out maxims and excuses for "playing it safe and staying in place" are replaced by a more proactive posture.

As widespread buy-in among managers and staff occurs, individually and collectively, everyone accepts the challenge of propelling business forward. In that regard, the business can experience the creation of value on many different levels. No matter how long the business has been in a holding state, great things can happen.

PEGs, however, are not magicians pulling rabbits out of hats. The practices and procedures they employ have existed for decades. The great strength of PEGs is their ability to coordinate and activate effective business practices that most small businesses, for whatever reason, have not embraced.

SEEKING THE RIGHT BUYER

The winnowing process that PEGs employ in deciding to acquire a company is mirrored by the one they use when getting ready to sell. They know in advance that the potential buyers for the company they've acquired will also follow rigorous procedures in evaluating the business.

How do PEGs identify the best buyers? Long before they acquire a business, PEGs develop a roster of prospective acquirers, just as they have a roster of subject matter experts. PEG managers know in advance who are the larger entities in a particular industry.

Some of the contacts they maintain are multiple acquirers. In other words, these are groups who constantly buy businesses in a particular industry. As with every industry, there are larger PEGs and smaller

Investment Money Abounds

Unbeknownst to most people, small businesses can attract vast sums of investment dollars, regardless of the apparent state of the economy. When you consider insurance company funds, the domestic and international pool of pension funds, the well of limited partner capital, institutional endowments, and private individual investment funds, all of which perpetually seek solid opportunities for growth in their investment dollars, it is humbling to realize that PEGs have raised more capital in the past several years than in all previous years since the industry's inception.

Cumulatively, PEGs have raised an excess of one trillion dollars in global capital, which, bolstered by several trillion dollars in the form of debt applied by banks and other lenders, makes the climate rosy for investment in businesses like yours. Across the board, the top PEGs enjoy excellent returns over time from the aggregate of their investments. Moreover, the best-performing PEGs are growing substantially. Long term, the percentage of small businesses owned by PEGs is increasing.

PEGs. The larger PEGs often buy from the smaller PEGs when the portfolio companies become sufficiently valuable that they meet the larger group's investment criteria. A handful of multi-billion-dollar private equity funds are well positioned to acquire almost any company they want. They establish a minimum investment criterion; for example, $50 million. In that case, they would be a prime prospective buyer for a small PEG that has grown its company to the size of $50 million.

Then there are the synergistic buyers. Synergistic buyers represent those who are either vertical or horizontal integrators within an industry. They are opportunistic. They expand their horizontal or vertical links when they recognize the value in, say, having their own manufacturer of a key part in their product, or need to strengthen their own distribution channel, or want to take advantage of a market opportunity. It's more difficult to find synergistic buyers, because they typically only search for a brief time. In contrast, PEGs are always buying.

In making acquisitions, a publicly traded company can be a synergistic buyer using its own stock as if it were currency. This maneuver can have tax advantages to the seller. However, publicly traded companies are more likely to use cash if their share price is too low.

When a PEG is ready to sell a company, it has everything in order so that potential buyers have all they need to effectively evaluate the company. The PEG will ensure that all current financial reports are available and that no buyer has any concern about undertaking financial due diligence. Audited statements by reputable CPA firms speak for themselves.

Anticipating potential buyers' needs in evaluating the company, the PEG takes care of as much as is practical in preparing for a possible sale. In doing so, the PEG lowers the financial risk profile of the company and saves potential acquirers significant time and investment in their evaluation.

LET'S REVIEW

A PEG acquires a business with an end goal in mind—to sell it for maximum value. The PEG defines what that end goal is and seeks to achieve it, free of personal and emotional attachment to the business. PEGs are able to make unbiased business decisions and are not fearful of spending money or incurring debt as needed because it is not personal debt. They are always on the lookout for value-maximizing opportunities.

Even if you have no intention of selling your business, or you've never contemplated doing so, the advantages of emulating the business practices of PEGs are countless. You can employ their methods to compete in the same markets against your fiercest competitors.

However, you will want to avoid the situation in which too many business owners find themselves: once they've gained and bought into insights for increasing value, they take a less-than-consistent and comprehensive approach to applying proven measures. Their business limps along in a state of underperformance, showing pockets of improvement here and there, but never truly reaching the significant potential that awaits. Don't let this happen to your company. The next chapter goes into the difference between successful PEG strategies and typical small business strategies in even more detail.

CHAPTER 4: WHAT PEGS DO THAT MOST BUSINESSES DON'T

To increase and preserve the value of a business, PEGs do many things differently than the typical business owner. The chart on page 59 briefly lists some of the PEGs' major offensive and defensive strategies for the companies they acquire. Business owners could reap significant benefits by implementing even a few things on this list.

Beneficial strategies can be adopted in several categories, including financial measures, protections, planning, expertise, and assessment. As you'll soon discover, the differences in how PEGs and the typical business approach these important areas can be dramatic.

FINANCIAL MEASURES

PEGs are focused on driving up the value of the companies they acquire. They are masters of enhancing valuation. In contrast, most small business owners are not aware of the array of strategies available. Strict control of financial statements, budgeting, a sale-oriented approach to taxes, access to capital, and debt management are all areas in which PEGs outperform the typical small business.

Audited statements. The quality, accuracy, and reliability of the financial statements upon which PEGs insist often outstrip what the typical private business is able to provide. Because PEGs have a fiduciary responsibility to their investors, and because they understand the value of third-party audited accounting statements and annual financial reports, PEGs attain a clear and accurate understanding of the true performance of their portfolio companies.

Each PEG portfolio company's performance is evaluated based on generally accepted accounting procedures (GAAP), so the group knows that both the revenue and the expenses are accurately accrued. A series of checks and balances is undertaken by the PEG's CPA firm and its auditors. The profit and loss statement is verified. With GAAP statements, plants and equipment are valued properly, and accompanying footnotes to any statement are complete. PEGs can depend on those documents, as can any other third party. They don't have to engage in any detective work to understand the company's financial performance.

In contrast, we have found almost without exception that non-audited private companies have inadequate financial statements, usually in that they do not properly allocate revenue and expenses for accrual-based accounting.

Real-time financial statements and performance metrics. PEGs insist on having up-to-the-minute accurate financial reporting that includes cash flow statements, net working capital, and profit and loss analysis by product line or service as well as consolidated for the enterprise. Management teams are trained to manage the business by the numbers, so it's essential that these statements be timely and accurate.

STRATEGIES FOR MAXIMIZING VALUE: TYPICAL PEGS VS. TYPICAL BUSINESS OWNERS

	PEG	Owner	Offensive or Defensive
Financial			
Annual audited financials	P		O/D
Focus on maximizing EBITDA	P		O/D
Budgeting and financial analysis	P		D
Strategic use of debt	P		O
Access and availability to capital	P		O
Focus on valuation	P		O
ROI and IRR analysis	P		O/D
Short-term tax strategies		P	D
Protections			
Employee non-compete agreements	P		D
Non-circumvention agreements	P		D
Arbitration/mediation clauses with vendors/ customers & employees/contractors	P		D
Intellectual property protection (patents, copyrights, trademarks)	P		D
Personal guarantees		P	O/D
Emotional ties to the business		P	O/D
Planning			
Succession planning	P		D
Catastrophic planning	P		D
Acquisition mindset concerning business, product lines	P		O/D
Best practices analysis and implementation	P		O
Long-term strategic planning	P		O/D
Exit strategy	P		D
Expertise			
Expert board of directors	P		O/D
Access to subject matter and niche experts	P		O/D
Talent search	P		O/D
Knowledge of ideal acquirers	P		O

	P		O/D
rvice analysis	P		O/D
...essment of recurring revenue opportunities	P		O
Cost and vendor analysis	P		D
Strength assessment	P		O
Weakness assessment	P		O/D
Continual competitive analysis	P		O/D
Continual opportunity assessment	P		O/D
Continual search for improvements	P		O
Focus on exploiting untapped opportunities	P		O

© *Bob Scarlata, 2012*

If issues arise (and they always do), it's critical to find out early to minimize harm and maximize opportunities.

PEGs also continually analyze and refine performance metrics. It's a closed loop feedback system: Measure results. Suggest changes to improve results. Implement. Measure results. Repeat. This feedback loop is only possible with real-time, accurate performance data that measure the right performance aspects.

Tax approaches that maximize profit. Taxes represent another difference in how PEGs and the typical private business owner operate. Many business owners believe that it's in their best interest to maximize their personal income by taking steps that artificially decrease taxes. On the face of it, that doesn't sound so bad. Long term, however, seeking to decrease tax obligations can make the business's earnings look lower than they actually are and diminish the resulting multiple valuation that the business might otherwise achieve upon sale.

For example, we worked with a client in a defense-related industry located in the southeast who had taken an ill-advised step during the process of selling his company. He rolled the revenue of the current year into the next year by delaying billings, thus decreasing earnings for the year in question. The current year's EBITDA was to be used as the multiplier for the selling price. Unfortunately, he undertook this maneuver during the due diligence phase. While he avoided nearly $100,000 in taxes, he lost $1.1 million in the selling price. Had he not engaged in this reshuffling, his overall gain would have been greater than ten to one. This strategy also severely damaged his credibility and resulted in a lower multiple paid for the business. (When you hear such a story, it defies belief. But we were there. We witnessed this. This type of error happens repeatedly, more often than not, with privately held businesses—owners routinely pick up pennies and step over dollars.)

Budgeting. Most business owners don't have an annual budget, and many have no clear idea of projected earnings over the next twelve months. They haven't scouted sales pipelines to determine what kind of revenues might be on the horizon. On the expense side of the ledger, they haven't thought through what costs they'll be incurring throughout the year.

This behavior might seem naive, but I assure you that these are not seat-of-the-pants entrepreneurs. They simply do not take the time to formulate a yearlong revenue and expense projection. The irony is that with readily available spreadsheet software, anyone can create a twelve-month cash flow statement, and most anyone can devise a three-year pro forma income statement. But business owners are often so caught up the in day-to-day activities of running their businesses that they don't look up, take their blinders off, and see what's coming down the pike. They're whacking through the weeds in the valley, giving no attention to the mountain that looms on the horizon.

By contrast, PEGs vigilantly engage in budgeting of all kinds. They undertake cash flow analysis for twelve, thirty-six, and even sixty months. They devise pro forma statements for one to three years or more. They employ a variety of financial measures and analyses to better manage the business. PEGs are comfortable and familiar with cash flow analyses and pro forma statements, sources and uses of funds analysis, and other financial measures, whereas many small business owners are not. Even if they know how to employ software tools to help with these measures, they often simply never do.

Cost analysis. Similarly, the typical business owner is not aware of the cost of the company's products and services, but PEG managers insist on knowing this information. By having accurate, up-to-the-minute cost data available, PEG managers sometimes can achieve dramatic increases in profitability, as a result of 1) dropping products and services that aren't carrying their weight and 2) finding more efficient ways to produce those products and services that generate healthy revenues.

Many business owners routinely use the same suppliers, same utilities services, the same this, and the same that. They don't rigorously determine if they're still working with the best vendors, getting the best deals, or following the best procedures. PEGs have no qualms about replacing a supplier, changing over the accounting system, upgrading or dropping products, or even dropping certain customers, if the cost of serving them is prohibitive.

If you don't know the true cost of supplying a customer or of supplying certain products or services, how do you know which ones are pulling their weight versus those that actually contribute little to revenue and profitability?

Debt management. Business owners typically regard debt as a necessary evil, whereas PEGs consider it to be a vital tool.

The typical business owner who needs to incur debt is often in trouble. Perhaps the business is not operating efficiently, or revenues are lagging. Either way, a cash flow analysis, which could have pinpointed potential cash flow deficits, usually has not been prepared. When a small business owner incurs debt, it's often with associated pain and suffering that PEGs do not experience. PEG managers do not have to sign personally for a loan; owners do.

Often, the bank or lender wants a co-signature from the business owner's spouse. Worse, the lender may ask for security interest in the owner's home. Banks want to be over-collateralized. As a matter of policy, banks do not lend funds to smaller companies without obtaining personal guarantees from the owner.

PEGs use debt judiciously. They have no desire to put their investment funds at risk. When PEGs acquire debt for one of their portfolio companies, it is a calculated financial maneuver designed to accomplish a specific objective. When a PEG acquires a company, it has used debt to make that acquisition. Referred to as senior debt, this includes funds expended on machinery, equipment, furniture, and fixtures. Lines of credit are established for the net working capital of the business, i.e., the company's inventory and receivables. PEGs may also use debt to expand or improve the business in the form of additional lines of working capital for increased accounts receivable and inventory financing. When PEGs use debt to increase the company's value, it is called leverage.

Banks have a completely different orientation when making loans to PEGs. Bankers know they're going to receive audited financial statements. It's likely they've worked with PEGs before and know that they take a disciplined approach to growing their businesses.

> If your business is poised for growth and the mere thought of acquiring debt disturbs you, you could be an excellent candidate for acquisition.
>
> The debt that the PEG acquires to help fuel your business is likely to lead to operating efficiencies, greater revenues, or both, which ultimately leads to the sale of your business at a multiple you never imagined.

In addition, they know that PEGs might want to help the company grow by coming back to the well and borrowing again. Thus, bankers routinely lend to PEGs without requesting any personal guarantees.

The lenders to which the PEGs are indebted have covenants, which can include working capital ratios such as current assets versus current liabilities. If the company breaks a covenant, then the loan can be called, placing the company in jeopardy. Because the typical PEG's business acquisition strategy depends upon effectively using leverage, and leverage entails incurring debt, PEGs are required by third-party lenders to exercise a fair amount of discipline. The typical owner doesn't want to incur debt, often because he or she doesn't understand the principle of leverage. However, this leads to slower growth, missed opportunities, and a lower rate of return.

Access to capital. Suppose a PEG has an interest in acquiring a business that has significant opportunities for growth. The PEG has a pool of capital available to invest. If the best way to earn the highest return is to invest more equity in the acquisition, the PEG will proceed with that strategy.

In general, PEGs have considerable access to capital. Suppose a PEG acquires a manufacturing firm and determines that opening a new facility in another part of the country or the world is prudent. In that instance, the PEG may not be able to borrow the funds needed for additional investment. Fortunately, it will have capital to draw on and can even raise additional capital if needed. Hence, the business receives a cash injection unlike anything the owner could muster.

If the owner can't raise that kind of capital, certainly not in a tight time frame, and is reticent or unable to borrow needed money, no expansion will occur. The difference between PEGs and business owners in relation to capital is stark: business owners cannot capitalize on the opportunities that the PEG managers regard as a perfect fit in the overall strategy of maximizing the business's value.

PROTECTIONS

Another area in which PEGs exhibit superior knowledge and practice is in the area of protecting businesses from risk. Many middle-market businesses are operating without protection against lawsuits, reputation damage, and competition from former employees. PEGs, on the other hand, wouldn't dream of running a business without these.

Employee non-compete agreements. PEGs insist on having employees in a small business venture sign a non-compete agreement. Many small business owners have never even heard of the document, let alone asked anyone to sign one. My company, the March Group, has lost deals when the businesses with whom we were working did not have non-compete agreements.

For example, we lost one deal with a manufacturing company in the southeast when a 10 percent partner who was also an officer in the company suddenly departed. With no non-compete agreement in place, this partner launched his own company, lifted our client's customer database, took the biggest customer away, and wreaked havoc. The 90 percent owner had no recourse against him; without a documented non-compete agreement, he could not obtain an injunction to stop the wholesale raiding of the customer database. The company that had been contemplating acquiring our client pulled up stakes and rode into the sunset.

If only that were the worst we've seen. We also know of instances where employees have cornered the owner by essentially saying, "Unless you pay me X amount of money, I'm going to relocate to this rival company." What is an owner to do in such circumstances? If this is a key employee, perhaps someone of long and loyal service who has been lured by a mega-dollar offer from a bitter rival… Well, you know where this is going.

Ironically, the best opportunity for a business owner to issue a non-compete agreement is when first hiring someone. Candidates are generally eager to land their jobs. Years later, after they gain some expertise and develop contacts, they begin to think, "I could do a better job at this myself," or "Hey, I might be worth more at a competitor." The non-compete agreement they nonchalantly signed years back can be important to the employer's long-term existence.

When owners hear about the need to enforce non-compete agreements, the first question they often have is, "How do I obtain these retroactively?" Fortunately, there are ways of accomplishing this task. Different states have different laws regarding non-compete agreements.

Non-circumvention agreements. Non-circumvention means that an employee cannot depart your company for a competitor and then approach your customers. This differs to some degree from a typical non-compete agreement and can be easier to implement and to enforce with current employees. As with non-compete agreements, PEGs insist on these for employees in their acquisitions.

With such an agreement, it is wise to include a clause preventing any employee from hiring other company employees after joining another firm. Suppose a few of your employees decide to depart and start their own firm. They reason, "Maybe we can recruit Joe from production and Tracy from finance." This happens in consulting and engineering firms all the time. People branch off, and the first thing they often do when staffing up is recruit people they already know, namely, your employees. You want to ensure that ex-company members cannot raid your current staff in this way.

At this point, you might be among those who say, "An employee non-compete/non-circumvention agreement? I don't want to go down this path. It's like adding a layer of bureaucracy." Actually, not much is involved, and the protection it affords is more than worth the effort.

Arbitration and mediation. When a workplace issue becomes heated and ends up in court, the only ones who win are the lawyers. Everyone else loses. PEGs ensure that mediation/arbitration clauses are included in all non-compete and other employee agreements.

In mediation, the two disagreeing parties sit down at a table with a third party, known as a mediator. This person merely serves as a facilitator for conversation between the two parties. The mediator has no jurisdiction, legal standing, or authority. The mediator simply helps both sides discuss an issue and hopefully derive a workable agreement.

If mediation doesn't work, you can move onto arbitration. Arbitration means that each party presents their case to a single arbitrator or an arbitration board. The arbitrating authority decides on a course of action based on the testimony heard and issues a ruling. In the case of binding arbitration, that ruling carries the same weight as a courtroom ruling. One of the additional pluses associated with binding arbitration is that once the decision is made, there is no appeal. It's over.

Many attorneys believe that arbitration is worse for their clients than going to court. The reader must decide that. Although my experience is limited, I'd rather have a mediocre arbitration decision than a great courtroom decision. In court, even if you win, you lose, because of lawyer fees, negative publicity, bad will, and associated disruptions and distractions. Arbitration generally saves you significant time and money.

PLANNING

The reason PEGs are adamant on instituting protections in their businesses is that PEGs have a forward-thinking posture. They are always thinking about what might be coming down the road. As a result, they also outperform most middle-market business owners in planning for succession, catastrophes, long-term operations, and exit.

Succession planning. If few small business owners seek to have audited statements, engage in annual budgeting, or employ debt for purposes of leverage, even fewer address the topic of succession planning.

All companies, large and small, need to have sufficient bench strength. Turnover today is higher than in previous eras. People don't have the same kind of loyalty to their employers that they had years ago, and vice versa. A business must be prepared to lose good people at any time. It's not *if* it will happen, it's *when.*

A succession plan ensures that you have a manager in place with supporting lieutenants and people on the floor who understand their roles and responsibilities. A succession plan considers such vital questions as, "Who are our key people? What happens if we lose them? What opportunities do we provide for people to move up in the organization? How do we help motivate them to perform better?"

Succession planning might also entail acquiring "key man" insurance, to guard against the loss of a key employee. The way some small businesses are structured, if a key person departs, the company may be exposed to great financial risk.

The entrepreneur who never gets sick, who makes do whether or not key staff show up on any given day, might never have spent a single minute on the topic of succession planning. PEGs consider this issue intently.

Catastrophic planning. Suppose your plant happens to be in a tornado zone. What's your plan to evacuate staff on short notice? How will people be taken care of in the event of an emergency? If you're located anywhere in the state of Florida (or anywhere on the Gulf or Atlantic coasts), what are your emergency plans for hurricanes? What's your game plan if you lose electricity, water, and other utilities? How do you plan to get back up and running?

Many business owners neglect this type of planning. They are aware they should do it, but the day-to-day activities of running the business keeps them putting it off. PEGs, however, are aware that such plans can help preserve the value of the companies they acquire, and they make sure they are put in place.

Long-term strategic planning. The typical business owner likely has the capability to engage in some form of long-term strategic planning, but—as with financial planning—rarely does. Here's a quote from *Alice In Wonderland*: "If you don't know where you're going, any path will take you there." But it might turn out that "there" is not where you want to be.

In contrast, long-term strategic planning is an essential element of each acquisition for PEGs. Instead of following Alice down the rabbit hole, PEGs follow the advice of Steven Covey's *The Seven Habits of Highly Successful People:* "Start out with the end goal in mind."

A long-term strategic plan has a variety of elements. In fact, strategic planning involves so many components that it could be (and is) the subject of many books on its own. It often includes an analysis of return on investments from capital expenditures, a focus on business-development strategy (including an in-depth look at the marketing pipeline), an assessment of new prospects, strategies for closing on new prospects as well as existing customers, strategies for diversifying the customer base, and an examination of long-standing and potential new suppliers.

PEG managers closely examine those elements of a business that, ideally, business owners should be looking at all along. And in doing so, they virtually ensure conditions improve. Taking a

69

systematic approach to, say, business development almost guarantees that you're going to do better than otherwise. Once you have a strategy in place for further developing new prospects, you're going to have a better sales year.

Exit strategy. The typical business owner rarely, if ever, thinks about an exit strategy, or how he or she is going to depart the business. PEGs never lose sight of their exit strategy. Exiting acquired businesses is what they're all about.

EXPERTISE

Unlike most middle-market business owners, PEGs are heavily focused on evaluating and acquiring the best talent for their companies. Unburdened by misplaced loyalties or habits, they can recruit and retain the best people to advise and improve the companies they acquire.

Board of directors. When PEGs acquire a business, they fill the board of directors with industry and other subject matter experts. They draw upon their key contacts to ensure that a vibrant, forward-thinking board is in place to propel the company during the PEG's tenure. They closely involve board members in the activities and affairs of the company.

The small-venture entrepreneur might or might not have a board of directors, depending on whether the business is a sole proprietorship, a partnership, or some type of corporation. Small businesses incorporated by law have boards, but they pale in comparison to the composition and effectiveness of boards that PEGs assemble for the companies that they acquire. Any business owner could have an advisory board of directors that meets on a predetermined basis to discuss and review critical issues of the business. Few small business owners in proprietorships or partnerships ever assemble such an advisory board. Even when they do, most don't employ the board to an optimal degree.

As discussed elsewhere in this book, PEGs also have access to a roster of niche and subject matter experts that far exceeds anything the typical business owner can assemble. PEGs will draw on such experts and pay their fees if doing so supports the overall direction they've plotted for the business.

Scouting for talent. Many successful businesses maintain a posture of interviewing all the time, whether or not there's a current need. It makes good sense to know who's available and to know what skills you can draw upon if the need arises. A strong database of contacts helps. If you run into big problems, you know where to turn.

PEGs invest in the people within the companies they acquire. They would prefer to keep the founder/owner in place after the acquisition. They would prefer to maintain other key managers and staff. PEG managers have a keen eye on the talent within a small business enterprise. They know too well what kinds of problems can occur following the departure of a key player within a company. PEGs are aware of who's been on board, for how long, and in what capacity they serve.

ASSESSMENT

When you're a business owner, you often don't have the time to take a step back and really evaluate your business. You're too busy with day-to-day stuff—meeting deadlines, putting out fires, etc. But PEGs know that an aerial view of the company's strengths, weaknesses, revenue streams, and products and services is essential to capturing opportunities that will increase the company's value.

Strength assessment. Our long-term experience in working with many successful privately owned companies is that owners, and sometimes firms' key lieutenants, represent a wealth of great ideas. Although some ideas actually get developed, most sit on a shelf. Either owners lack the time, energy, or inclination to follow through, or they become risk averse.

While many people view entrepreneurs as modern-day swashbucklers who boldly venture forth, this usually isn't the case. Even a bold entrepreneur or business owner finds that he/she is satisfied with performance as it is and abstains from further investment(s) in growth opportunities. If the business has been up and running for a while, and earnings have been consistent, why tip the apple cart? Why reach for some new carrot that could have a big payoff but will require much in terms of time, energy, and investment? Many owners do not bother to capitalize on one of their greatest strengths: the ability to generate potentially profitable ideas.

PEGs, in contrast, want to know about those ideas, take them off the shelf, and assess their viability. Which ideas have the highest revenue and earning potential? To find out, they create a priority list, proceed down that list, and make key assessments. Which ideas are closest to fruition? Which hold the greatest overall potential? Which offer supreme leverage based on what the company is already providing?

In this respect, a change of ownership (i.e., being acquired by a PEG), represents a breath of fresh air. For the first time in perhaps years, a business is put back on the path to achieving much of its potential.

Weakness assessment. Assessing their personal weaknesses is territory to which many business owners never travel. Or, they will attempt to strengthen their weaknesses themselves, which generally proves to be fruitless—studies show that you're better off acquiring expertise in an area where you are weak than devoting significant time and effort to personally shoring it up.

If I am not good at creating websites, for example, and have no flair for the art, I could spend the next ten years figuring out how to be a better web designer. However, it would be faster, easier, and more efficient for me to stick with those areas where I am strong and to bring in somebody who is skilled at web design.

Some business owners feel as if they have sufficient knowledge of manufacturing processes, so they flounder around, seeking to improve end results, all because they don't want to spend $9,500 to retain an expert who can provide highly competent services and rapidly offer the right type of guidance. Such entrepreneurs could have earned more revenue by sticking with their strengths during the time they dabbled around in an area where they had no business engaging in the first place.

One of the weaknesses we typically see among business owners is a short-term orientation, to the detriment of the long term. Owners are concerned about how much cash is in the bank account, as opposed to the PEG manager, who is concerned about the value the business will rise to on the day it is put up for resale.

The owner might not want to decrease his bank account by $9,500 to hire a manufacturing expert, whereas the PEG manager won't think twice about the prospect if it points to a rosier future. The PEG is more than willing to invest and reinvest in the company on a short-term basis, even when it knows that such an investment will not make profits in the short term, as long as the investment maximizes profits and value in the long term and leads to a more lucrative sale.

Recurring revenue. When acquiring a privately held company, PEGs examine recurring revenue opportunities and regard them as a critical component of the acquisition. Can a product or service be offered on a cyclical basis, such as monthly, quarterly, semi-annually, or annually? Can add-ons to a project be dispensed at regular intervals? What avenues are available to create annuity types of revenue streams? The higher the percentage that recurring revenue contributes to a company's overall revenues, the more valuable that company could prove to be to a PEG and to the next buyer, too.

It's one thing to land a big contract that requires many first-time types of activities and to feel proud about your accomplishment. Does this contract, however, lead to others? That is a key concern of PEG managers.

While many small business owners overlook the opportunity for maintenance agreements, service agreements, royalty revenues, and whatever else links the customer to the business on a routine basis, PEGs are keen at the outset to examine such possibilities. The greater the continuity of income, the more easily they can predict future income, and the more interested PEGs become in a company.

Predictable revenues contribute to the ultimate value of the company and the multiple at which it sells. It also lowers the business's risk profile, which in turn raises the multiple.

Product and service analysis. Related to all the above, business owners are reluctant to raise prices. Owners get comfortable, to some degree, with the prices they charge for their various products or services. Some feel that a price rise would drive business away and that they would no longer be competitive. Because they haven't undertaken a rigorous product and service analysis, they have little idea as to what the market can bear.

By contrast, a PEG will undertake a thorough market analysis on each product and each service to determine the price that will result in the highest revenue and contribution margin.

PEGs know that an effective increase in price yields a direct incremental increase in the bottom line, given that costs stay constant. They also know that retitling a product or service, repackaging it, or bundling it with something else might make a big difference in

74

revenue. Owners rarely look outside their day-to-day concerns to explore these options.

In most small businesses, as in much of life, 20 percent of the product or service offerings yield 80 percent of earnings. This is the 80-20 rule, or the Pareto Principle. Some business owners get caught up in offering the same mix of products or services because they believe that's what customers want, or they seek to be a full-service provider, even if the delivery of some of those services cripples the business. One symptom of this: some owners feel it's vital to have a website that goes on for pages and pages, offering product and service descriptions and explaining everything the business can do. But the best website offering might be just five or six pages, highlighting an optimal mix of profitable products and services, as revealed by product and service analysis.

DEFENSIVE STRATEGIES: PEGS AVOID LAND MINES, AND YOU CAN, TOO

Avoiding land mines requires defensive strategies, many of which are unknown or never undertaken by small business owners.

Human resources management: a lurking powder keg. In your company, does everyone precisely understand the federal government rules and regulations about discrimination (particularly racial or sexual)? Do you have an employee handbook that details all of the company's personnel policies and procedures? Is your handbook continually updated with current federal and state regulations? Is it distributed to employees and discussed when they are first hired or as a part of orientation? Is this guide discussed periodically throughout the year so that everyone remains current in their knowledge of what represents acceptable behavior and practice and what does not? If not, you may have an unnecessarily high risk of lawsuit. And the more successful a business is, the more vital these otherwise tedious tasks become.

PEGs are keen to ensure that policy and procedures manuals are current and in the possession of all company staff. Via continual training and policy directives, they keep employees alert to the pitfalls of engaging in behavior that could prompt a discrimination suit. They are willing to bring in outside experts when an issue arises, and they don't let matters fester. With their roster of contacts and experts, they have access to the best and most current advice for your jurisdiction, county, and state.

Safety and health considerations. Safety can have a huge impact on costs (particularly when it comes to workers' compensation claims), not to mention the lives and health of everyone in your company. You can't avoid this issue. PEGs approach it with special care. Questions they consider include: If the business involves any type of manufacturing, production, trucking, shipping, or other physical activity, has a worker disability insurance program been put in place? What about proactive measures to support the health and well-being of employees? Does the business encourage employees to join health clubs, enroll in exercise classes, or take diet and nutrition counseling? Are such benefits provided as part of the overall compensation plan? Alternatively, does the business maintain higher deductibles on health insurance policies? Would it be better to design a self-insurance program instead of paying into programs designed by insurance companies?

With most business owners, fear of getting hit in the pocketbook helps them to be more willing to make changes. Otherwise, they're likely to pay little or no attention to safety and employee health. But PEG managers subscribe to that old maxim "an ounce of prevention is worth a pound of cure."

Defensive competitive analysis. Because PEGs invest in a business for a three- to five-year stretch, they want to know what's occurring in the marketplace, specifically with the company's customers, suppliers, and competitors. All three areas represent potential risks to the business.

The activities of competitors, in particular, can be hidden financial land mines. PEGs are willing to invest in obtaining a competitive analysis that highlights opportunities and risks. They're well aware that a competitor with a superior product or service offering, better procedures, or an enhanced market position can broadside an unsuspecting business. PEGs know the top marketing analysts and will retain them at critical junctures.

In contrast, business owners might be aware of their competitive shortcomings. Some even know the hazards of ignoring this issue. Still, they don't want to pay the experts that could illuminate a situation and help put them on the proper path.

When PEGs bring in experts, there's no doubt that they will do the job, because they have performed admirably over and over again. When business owners get around to bringing in someone, if ever, it's often the wrong person. So they waste money and time and are misdirected—a triple loss.

Defensive tax practices. Taxes are an inevitable cost of doing business—one that dogs entrepreneurs every step of the way. Business owners often run into problems with the IRS because they don't put aside enough money for their quarterly taxes. Many seem to scramble about as the end of the tax quarter draws near. They need to make a huge sale to raise the funds that they should have been socking away all along. Then, it all starts again with next quarter's tax payment. Being perpetually short on tax payments is related to improper cash flow planning, accounting, and budgeting—activities in which PEGs frequently engage.

PEGs maintain a wide perspective about tax issues. As with competitive analysis and other aspects of the business, PEGs won't hesitate to bring in a tax specialist to ensure that they have the best advice and are able to avoid paying excess taxes that can drain funds away from the business. Every dollar a business legitimately retains ultimately contributes to the multiplier effect on the value of the business.

All businesses face a multitude of taxes, including sales taxes, excise and franchise taxes, state income taxes, and federal taxes. Any tax can have a significant impact on the business and its opportunity to maximize the after-tax net gain. Often, tax experts will save you more money than it costs to bring them in, and in many instances, they will save you a multiple of their fee.

Reputation management: it's a complainer's market. With the rise and prominence of the Internet, reputation management has become a huge issue. Virtually every company today has a website, and most have an Internet marketing strategy, which generally represents a prudent, proactive way of doing business. Sadly, one single disgruntled employee or one unhappy customer can do great harm to a company's reputation in a matter of minutes.

Often, the harm is entirely undeserved. The complainer could be an irrational person who doesn't even want to resolve the problem. Untold numbers of people use the Internet as a salve for all things that have gone wrong in their lives or careers. The ease with which they can create anonymous email accounts prompts them to throw darts and daggers at the targets that have rankled them. If you haven't been affected by a malicious attack thus far, consider yourself lucky.

Unfortunately, the Internet does not have a reboot feature. When someone posts an exceedingly critical comment on a high visibility social networking website or on one of the myriad consumer opinion sites, their words reverberate around the web forever. Someone who looks up your company is likely to find this negative information, no matter how much positive information is out there, too. Regardless of the validity or the accuracy of the claims, the damage to your reputation can cost you millions of dollars, depending on what type of business or industry you're in, who your customers are, and how new prospects find you.

78

Business owners often lack the time, energy, or requisite knowledge to protect their reputations proactively, before real trouble hits the fan. Some naively believe that they can effectively address negative posts about them and solve the issue. But when you interact with a disgruntled party online, often you simply fan the flames. That person responds with greater vigor, and now you've raised the potential that the squabble will rise in the search engine rankings.

Consider the scenario where everything that another party says about your company is a lie, and you can prove it, so you sue them. If the other party is well heeled, they can subpoena all of your documentation, which means that it will go public. The legal costs will be staggering. The case will go on for years. Management resources will be drained. The legal dispute itself may be the lead search engine hit when someone seeks information about your company.

Unquestionably, the best option to this real and likely land mine is to build a moat around your reputation before it comes under attack. PEG managers know the extreme importance of building a moat around the websites of the companies they own. They hire reputation management experts to create positive press and to ensure that anyone who uses a search engine to look up information on one of their acquired companies will find positive press on at least the first page of the returns, if not page after page.

I was blind, but now I see. If you're like most business owners, by now you begin to realize that you've been operating all these years without a net. You've invested your time, energy, and funds, perhaps while neglecting your family, leisure activities, and even health, and have thrown everything into the business.

With eyes wide open, you now understand that events have gone marvelously well, considering everything that could go wrong. Alas, you have no guarantee that from this day forward, you can avoid the issues presented here. As revealed in this interview with

Tim Butler, how you manage directly impacts whether or not you run into financial difficulties.

INTERVIEW: GOOD MANAGEMENT, FINANCIAL FEASIBILITY

Before he launched Growth Fire, Tim Butler was CEO of a privately held software company with roughly 278 shareholders and, as he calls it, a convoluted capital structure. He has much to share about avoiding land mines.

Bob: What was your situation in the software company?

Tim: The company had been in the market for seventeen years and was struggling. Investors had expectations, were seeking to exit at some point, and the company just wasn't providing it. I inherited a suboptimal, almost bust situation; they had cash flow, but it wasn't great.

Bob: Were you able to effect an exit?

Tim: No. The product was good but not high on anyone's list. People weren't saying, "I've got to buy this." We sold through an original equipment manufacturer to Fortune 500 firms for $100 to $250 per copy, but if you want to build a company that has some size and can provide a return, you've got to sell high-value products. So we refocused, sold the applications that the product could deliver rather than selling the product itself, and built a direct sales force to support that.

We dramatically changed direction and started selling applications for $100,000 to $750,000 per solution. Unfortunately, a significant change in the board of directors occurred, and the remaining board wanted to revert to the original model, focusing on technology rather than solutions the market was seeking. Since then, the company has been declining in revenue, hanging on with no one able to prosperously exit.

Prior to that, I was part of a turnaround team assisting the current owners in an enterprise resource planning company. The company was in the $16 million to $17 million range, with roughly break-even profitability. We solved some of the company's core problems and, within three years, we raised sales to $20 million plus and in excess of $2.5 million EBITDA. We were able to sell the company in an all-cash transaction. Our job was to cover the basics: get the product aligned and make sure they are executing.

Before that experience, I had launched a start-up out of my basement in customer relationship management (CRM) for small and medium businesses. We got some outside funding, acquired a product, and were determined to launch a CRM system into the marketplace. We grew to fifteen employees before we moved into a formal office space.

We clearly had a good product, but right after 2000, the market was running against us. We ended up selling that company by preparing to be acquired, and then we helped run the dot-com that acquired the company.

Bob: The premise of this book is that PEGs are "sellers" from day one.

Tim: So true. I've got a blog entry on the Growth Fire blog about how PEGs look at companies. Everything that PEGs can bring to the table is available to the business owner, with one exception: cash. But cash is a symptom; it's not a problem.

PEGs reputedly are better at financial management, but that's not where they get their gains. Their long-term gains are from operational excellence. And it is through such operational excellence that PEGs avoid financial land mines.

Every company has operational excellence available to them. It's a management, as well as a leadership, issue. If you're a business owner, you know your industry and your clients' needs better than anybody, and likely better than PEGs. But PEGs can step back and distance themselves from the problem. They are practiced at doing that.

Passion and focus make an entrepreneur successful. Oftentimes, though, they can trip up an entrepreneur who continues to push a bad situation rather than stepping back and saying, "This isn't working. I've got to try something else." So you see too many owners, particularly in the emerging software market, who think that if they can get a company to $5 to $15 million from a technology standpoint, then they can get enough buyers in the market. But you can't build a company over the long term if you can't figure out how you're going to work on the business versus working on the technology.

PEGs will say, "We're not here to focus on technology, we're here to build a business." Their focus is on execution, operations, alignment with the market, alignment with the customer needs, and solving the problems. Often you hear: "If only the market understood what we've got." You're asking the market to do a lot of work. Instead, you have to focus on helping the market understand how you can solve their problem. That's a different conversation than saying, "Listen, I have a great technology."

Bob: What are you currently pursuing?

Tim: Growth Fire is a private equity-backed firm focused on finding software companies with unrealized potential at a fair value to our firm. An ideal company for us earns $10 to $20 million in revenue, with $1 to $2 million in EBITDA. It has good foundations and is likely at a transition point without the necessary thinking or elements to get through that process. The owner could be tired and thinking, "I've run this company for twenty years, and I've got it up to $15." Such owners don't get enough respect; they've taken a tremendous risk and have worked their tails off to reach that point.

Bob: Entrepreneurs take a tremendous amount of risk—define what that means.

Tim: You're dealing with scarce resources to launch a company and then high risk to make it past the first five years. Eighty percent of companies will fail within their first five years. Entrepreneurs often put their life savings and all of their passion into the venture, working probably twelve to fourteen hours a day for the first five years to get this company launched. That's a lot of risk for the 20 percent return they'll likely get at the end. If they bring the company to $5 to $10 million in annual revenue, they dream of $100 million.

The risks are all around: Can you find the right people? Can you build the right product? Is the market favorable? Are the indicators positive? Will a big company come along and squash me as soon as I get the company built? If I build this cool technology, will someone say, "I've already got a patent for it?"

Bob: So you're seeking to acquire a firm with good foundations in technology that is at an inflection point but that hasn't achieved its business potential. What will you bring to the table to enable such a company to achieve that full potential?

Tim: Most entrepreneurs actually don't want to build companies; they want to build technologies or products. Building a company requires human capital management, financial management, and market alignment. We bring in a different type of management leadership and development. We examine the business model and perhaps put a new model in place. Maybe the old competencies aren't working anymore; maybe a new set of competencies needs to be in place. Not to say that management and leadership in the past was bad, but rather a new type is now required.

We ensure that the products, technologies, organizational capabilities, and competencies are focused on the right market opportunities. A company on one trajectory has a different financial picture than a company on another trajectory. It's all about building the right framework and having the right alignment between all of the partners. In other words, you've got to pull apart the framework and reassemble it in a different way. Whether a company is acquired by a strategic partner or a PEG or it eventually goes public, a company experiences many transitions from its initial startup to its eventual outcome.

Bob: Yes, as a PEG, you are building the company for an exit. What are the characteristics that PEGs find desirable when they decide to buy?

Tim: PEGs look for strong markets and good management teams that demonstrate that they can execute, because execution trumps strategy. If you're in a decent market and you've got a good management team that can execute, they don't have to be strategic wizards. A good management team that converts resources into results trumps strategy every day.

Bob: The execution is continued growth and profitability of the company.

Tim: Yes. It's hard to change the headwind in an industry. But if you put a good management team in a decent industry, they'll do well relative to the industry. PEGs strive to assemble a good management team in an emerging, safe market.

Bob: What's the positive result of being superior to your competition in a good industry?

Tim: Higher growth and better and more predictable performance. If you're Groupon right now, or a Groupon competitor, and you're growing at 100 percent a year, it's hard to separate management from industry performance because the industry growth is overshadowing everything. In an industry that's growing at 10 percent per year, a company growing at 20 percent per year is doing something different and better than others.

Putting processes in place that offer some level of predictability is vital. Management teams that can deliver results are fine, but if you don't know where the results are coming from, that's not execution. I'll never back away from good luck, but you want to back up luck with good processes, sound business management, and an understanding of how you put it all together.

Bob: In terms of what PEGs see, many business owners don't put processes and steps into place. They don't understand the customer buying process and how it aligns with their selling process and the product or service they're offering.

Tim: Right. Owners have an inside-out focus rather than an outside-in focus. They proceed thinking, "Here's what we need to do, so let's go push this," without considering how people buy, where the market is, what real opportunity is, and how they can align themselves with that. The entrepreneur says, "Let's make it happen," in the face of all the danger. That's not how you build a business.

Bob: So entrepreneurs can choose, although they might not realize it. They can go it alone and attempt to sell out 100 percent, or they can take some chips off the table and align with a PEG.

Tim: As a former CEO sitting in a company, I would tell you that you would need to bring in outside capital and outside expertise if your organization is at a transition point in a rapidly growing industry. Conversely, if you had the capabilities within your company—the human resource capability as well as the financial wherewithal—to grow your company without bringing in outside investors, why would you give up equity?

Bob: In a fast-moving world, you either pounce on fleeting opportunities or you miss them. So, you find a suitable company and you build it up. At what point, and why, do you decide to exit?

Tim: You exit when you achieve the objectives that you initially set out to achieve. Many groups acquire companies with the idea they are going to exit in four years, but you can't see four years out. You can grow companies, but the company will sell when it's the right time for that company. Over a three- to four-year time frame, markets come and go, management and leadership come and go, and the economy goes up and down. One day somebody says, "What you've built has a lot of value, and we'd like to acquire it." So you look at your objectives and where the market is, and you think, "Is this a good offer for where we are right now, or do we believe we can do better?" Regardless of what you choose to do, you have to be in a ready state.

Bob: If you're not ready when that knock on the door comes, it might never come again.

Tim: Yes. Usually the first or second company in a market that sells gains the most value. Everybody else in that market is a follower, and you never get the same multiples. Ironically, the companies that are third, fourth, and fifth want to go after those multiples, and it's too late.

Bob: Although PEGs theoretically have a five- to ten-year window based on the life of their funds, they want to be ready to sell at all times because they don't know what the markets will bring in the future and because they have an obligation to their investors to capitalize on events as the occur.

Tim: That's exactly right. They've got to provide a 20 percent to 30 percent return to their investors on every investment.

Bob: The difference we see between PEGs and owners is that PEGs mentally are always ready to sell; business owners might not be ready, even if the business is.

Tim: An owner sees his future tied up in that company. PEGs see their future in a different way—they have the expectation to sell this company. That's one reason many deals fall apart at the very end. The guy sits down with his wife; he's got the term sheet in front of him, and he's got papers to sign, and he says, "I don't know what I'm going to do the day after tomorrow." The deal falls apart, and he ends up losing the potential value only because he didn't think about how to plan beyond that step.

That's the difference between being an owner with passion and looking dispassionately at the company and saying, "What do I need to do now to build this firm to greater value?"

Bob: How should they prepare?

Tim: They've got to be continually planning and contemplating the next big adventure. What happens if somebody comes in today and buys this company? Do they want to go to China and study art? Do they want to go back to school, start another company, become a philanthropist? Do they want to retire? Few prepare themselves for what's next. Part of the task is estate planning, part is transition planning, and part is life planning.

We looked at a company recently where the founder had already bought a house on the other coast, the family had already moved, his home was already up for sale, and he was talking about what he was going to do afterward. He had a high degree of comfort that he was going to sell. Then you talk to a guy whose wife doesn't know he's looking at selling the business. He doesn't know what he wants to do. There's a high likelihood that you're going to invest a lot of money into a deal that doesn't come to fruition.

Bob: Any other key perspectives to share?

Tim: Sure. First, few companies invest as much time or as many resources in building a company as building a product. Second, many companies operate on what I call a half-business model. For example, a distribution company might be good at the sales and marketing, but they don't create value.

Third, everybody has access to the same resources in the marketplace. Some people have the ability to capture and turn human capital into great results. They know how to turn people's heads and get them engaged—others don't. If you look at the differences in the companies that have capitalized on human capital and the ones that haven't, it is usually three-to four-fold.

Fourth, some companies deliberately create culture, but most companies have what I consider an "accidental" culture. They couldn't describe it, but it's there. They don't proactively think about how to create it and mold it.

Fifth, we've eliminated companies for consideration when valuation expectations were too different, when market opportunities were insufficient, when the degree of change needed represented too great a leap, and when we've asked for financials, say, three times over a six-week period.

Bob: Great insights!

Chapter 5: The Steps to a Sale

At this point you might be thinking, "Okay, you've convinced me. I'll get my business ready to sell and see what's out there. But what's the process? What can I expect?"

The process basically involves getting your financial statements ready, finding a buyer, and negotiating the deal. Within those three main activity areas, however, you will encounter a large number of complexities, many of which will require the assistance of professional intermediaries.

Getting Full Value: Recasting Financial Statements

As I discussed in Chapter 4, selling your business depends on having audited financial statements, including profit and loss, balance sheet, and income statements. You should develop these statements as a matter of course, whether you are selling your company or not. When you are selling, however, your focus must shift from minimizing taxes and maximizing personal benefits to increasing the valuation of your company in a sale.

The main indicator of value, to a PEG or other buyer, is earnings before interest, taxes, depreciation, and amortization, or EBITDA.

EBITDA is a framework that allows buyers to compare "apples to apples" instead of "apples to oranges" when viewing businesses with different operating structures. Recasting financial performance as it would be under management by PEG provides a clearer indication of EBITDA and more accurately reflects your company's true performance.

Recasting is the process of seeing the business with new eyes, as if someone else were operating it. Much of what's old and familiar to you is viewed from a new perspective. Your resources and inherent advantages are considered in terms of greater profit potential or exploration of new markets.

My company negotiated the sale of a business that was operating a large fleet of trucks. Suddenly, fuel prices shot up to unprecedented levels. We assessed the situation and found reason to believe that fuel prices would be more stable in the future. In preparing the profit and loss statement for EBITDA purposes, we recast the most recent fuel costs to more reasonable levels.

As a result of our analysis, the annual fuel costs were presented for the coming year as $500,000 less than earlier. That adjustment resulted in a $2 million increase in the business's valuation, and a buyer eventually bought the company based on that valuation. The buyer recognized that fuel prices represented an anomaly and that it was unrealistic to assess the company's true value when fuel prices were likely to return to a more stable level.

Chart 1, "Widget Manufacturing Company," presents a simplified profit and loss statement to highlight the crucial elements of EBITDA. In the example below, sales at calendar year end (CYE) are roughly $5.0 million, offset by $2.7 million in cost of goods sold, for a gross profit of $2.3 million. Deducting operating expenses of $1.2 million and manager's compensation of just above $100,000 for total expenses of $1.3 million, when subtracted from gross profit of $2.3 million, yields an EBITDA of just under $1 million, or $963,000.

Chart 1

Widget Mfg. Co., Inc. Summary of Earnings Before Interest, Taxes, Depreciation and Amortization December 31, XXXX		
		CYE
Sales		$5,035,363
Cost of Goods Sold		(2,727,476)
Gross Profit		2,307,887
Operating Expense		1,231,699
Manager's Compensation		113,000
Total Expense		1,344,699
EBITDA (Gross Profit - Total Expense)		$963,188

Income statement. Chart 2, Widget Manufacturing Company's income statement summary, expands upon Chart 1, showing additional components of cost of goods sold, operating expenses, and other income and expenses. The cost of goods sold is adjusted to reflect extraordinary, one-time expenses in that one year and to eliminate the depreciation the owner would claim on his or her taxes, thus presenting a more accurate picture of a purchaser's potential costs. Expenses are raised or lowered to account for changes in situation that would be experienced by a new owner.

Consider manager's compensation. Because the manager is the owner of the business, his compensation has not been negotiated at arm's length. If this same company were publicly traded, PEG managers would consider the true cost to compensate a high-quality manager on an arm's-length basis. Hence, while the extended profit and loss statement has no amount listed for a manager's compensation in the first CYE column, the adjustment is $113,000, and the recast statement for EBITDA purposes now includes that $113,000 sum.

We've had cases where a small business owner annually receives $500,000 in compensation, whereas the compensation in replacing him with a high-quality manager would equal $125,000. In evaluating

91

that business, the private equity group would add $375,000 to the bottom line—the amount saved when compensating the manager that the PEG would hire. Likewise, PEGs review all items that are listed (or that should be listed) in a company's profit and loss statement, and then determine what value to assign for EBITDA purposes.

As a result of Widget's recasting, the company's overall costs and expenses are lowered, and the EBITDA is thus raised from $580,226 to $963,187—a more than 60 percent increase. Which income statement makes the company look more attractive to a potential buyer?

Chart 2

Widget Mfg. Co., Inc. Income Statement Summary December 31, XXXX	CYE	Adjustments	Recast CYE	% of sales
Revenues				
Sales	5,035,363	0	5,035,363	100.00%
Total Sales	**$5,035,363**	**$0**	**$5,035,363**	**100.00%**
			0	
Cost of Goods Sold			0	
Cost of Goods Sold	2,876,908	(149,432)	2,727,476	54.17%
Depreciation	95,576	(95,576)	0	0.00%
Total Cost of Goods Sold	**$2,972,484**	**($245,008)**	**$2,727,476**	**54.17%**
GROSS PROFIT	**$2,062,879**	**$245,008**	**$2,307,887**	**45.83%**
Operating Expenses				
Manager's Compensation		113,000	113,000	2.24%
Salaries and Wages	646,808	(127,300)	519,508	10.32%
Payroll Taxes	44,672	(207)	44,465	0.88%
General Taxes and Licenses	1,640	0	1,640	0.03%
Rent	9,600	62,400	72,000	1.43%
Repairs and Maintenance	9,908	0	9,908	0.19%
Security System	471	0	471	0.01%
Legal and Accounting	6,294	0	6,294	0.12%
Advertising and Promotion	59,637	0	59,637	1.18%
Automotive	4,299	(3,224)	1,075	0.02%
Bank Service Charges	32,170	(10,000)	22,170	0.44%
Subscriptions and Memberships	960	0	960	0.02%
Insurance	58,034	0	58,034	1.15%
Consumables	3,683	0	3,683	0.07%
Utilities and Telephone	11,648	(582)	11,066	0.22%
Office Supplies and Expenses	12,815	0	12,815	0.25%
Supplies – Art and Shipping Dept.	51,429	(5,000)	46,429	0.92%
Postage and Delivery	3,221	0	3,221	0.06%
Supplies – Shipping Dept.	74,054	(74,054)	0	0.00%
Outside Services	480	0	480	0.01%
Travel	79,633	(15,927)	63,706	1.27%
Trash	777	0	777	0.02%
Bad Debts	1,961	0	1,961	0.04%
Cleaning	716	0	716	0.01%
Computer Expense	11,822	0	11,822	0.23%
Internet Expense	6,866	0	6,866	0.14%
Research and Development	3,518	0	3,518	0.07%

Freight and Postage	147,872	0	147,872	2.94%
Employee Recognition	3,426	0	3,426	0.07%
Education and Training	1,598	0	1,598	0.03%
Commissions Expense	105,851	0	105,851	2.10%
Equipment Rental	9,417	0	9,417	0.19%
Miscellaneous/Product Warranty	59,839	(58,625)	1,214	0.02%
Depreciation/Amortization	18,434	(18,434)	0	0.00%
Total Operating Expenses	$1,482,653	($137,953)	$1,344,700	26.69%
OPERATING INCOME	$590,226		$963,187	19.15%
Other Income (Expense)				
Interest Expense	(30,019)	30,019		0.00%
Income Taxes	(233,120)	233,120		0.00%
Total Other Income (Expense)	($263,139)	$263,139		0.00%
NET INCOME (LOSS)	$317,087			
EBITDA			$963,187	19.15%

Balance sheet. Balance sheets also offer perspective on a business's potential value. Chart 3 shows Widget Manufacturing's balance sheet summary. As shown in the notes, certain aspects of assets and liabilities have been adjusted to more accurately reflect their current value to the business. For example, cash and other items to be retained by the seller are subtracted from the business's assets, since they would not accrue to a purchaser. (Note: it's not unusual for a business owner, when selling his or her own business, to leave that cash on the balance sheet and to include it in the purchase price, thereby decreasing his or her total net proceeds.) The value of equipment is adjusted based on estimated fair market value on a going-concern, in-place basis, and the depreciation the seller would take off his or her taxes is subtracted to show the true value of the equipment to a purchaser. In addition, liabilities that the seller will retain are taken off the balance sheet, as the business would not have these at the time of sale (they'd be paid from proceeds).

In Chart 3, rent is listed as $9,600. In the adjustment column, rent is raised by $62,400, for a recast rent figure of $72,000. Why would an analyst allocate such a steep sum for rent? In this case, the business owner also owns the real estate on which the company sits. If *rent* for the premises were determined at arm's length, $72,000 would be realistic. Thus, the analyst "charges" the business more for this expense.

For shipping and supplies, the business owner's profit and loss statement shows an expense of $74,054. This was removed from operating expenses in the recast EBITDA calculation; that sum should have been associated with the cost of goods sold. This is an accounting issue, not a values issue.

All other adjustments, as reflected in Chart 3, represent reallocation or numerical changes based on a realistic assessment of the company's operating expenses. The analyst (a PEG, perhaps) is effectively saying, "If we were managing the company, this is what the income statement would look like and what the next acquirers will want to focus on."

Chart 3

Widget Mfg. Co., Inc.
Balance Sheet Summary
December 31, XXXX

	CYE	Adjustments	Recast CYE
Current Assets			
Cash	238,882 1	(238,882)	0
Accounts Receivable-Trade	546,092		546,092
Other Current Assets	20,422 4	(20,422)	0
Inventory	737,334		737,334
Total Current Assets	1,542,730		1,283,426
Fixed Assets			
Machinery and Equipment	1,795,431 2	(897,716)	897,715
Accumulated Depreciation	(1,257,690) 2	1,257,690	0
Net Fixed Assets	537,741		897,715
TOTAL ASSETS	2,080,471		2,181,141
Current Liabilities			
Accounts Payable-Trade	275,714		275,714
Accrued Expenses	24,554		24,554
Total Current Liabilities	300,268		300,268
Long-Term Liabilities			
LT Notes	280,000 3	(280,000)	0
Notes Payable	100,000 3	(100,000)	0
Total LT Liabilities	380,000		0
TOTAL LIABILITIES	680,268		300,268
Equity			
Common Stock	50,000		50,000
Retained Earnings	1,350,203		1,350,203
Recast Balancing Equity	0	480,671	480,671
Total Equity	1,400,203		1,080,874
TOTAL LIABILITIES & EQUITY	2,080,471		2,181,142

1 Assets retained by seller ($)
2 Recast to FMV of assets
3 Liabilities retained by seller
4 Employee advance – retained by seller

INTERVIEW: EBITDA DEMYSTIFIED

Rob Voeks started his career as a computer design engineer and has since worked for a number of companies and has seen many small companies grow from the ground up. Voeks attended The College of William & Mary to earn his MBA, and he later earned his PhD in corporate finance from the University of Georgia. He wrote his dissertation on the acquisition of privately held companies.

Following graduate school, Voeks worked at Matrix Capital for two and a half years, where he reviewed the financial structure and evaluation of many companies in a variety of industries. In January 2000, he joined Private Advisors, which is a fund of funds group that provides small companies with buyout funds. They have financially backed over fifty partnerships, which have collectively invested in more than five hundred companies. Voeks rose to become a principal of the firm, and today he understands better than most what makes a company attractive to private investment groups.

Bob: What do your best companies and partners do to maximize the eventual selling price of their company? What are the specific, actionable steps that they take once they buy a privately owned company?

Rob: Private equity returns originate from one of three areas. First, they can result from simply paying down debt. If a company with flat earnings adds financial leverage and pays debts, its equity value is going to increase.

Second is multiple expansion. You can purchase a company for four times EBITDA and ultimately sell that company for five or six times EBITDA. We believe that the market for privately held companies is relatively efficient. In today's environment, you generally get what you pay for.

95

Third is to increase cash flow, where EBITDA is roughly synonymous with cash flow. The best private equity funds grow the companies via top-line growth, cost cutting, or synergistic effort. That way, the company generates more cash at the end of a period of a private equity investment than when the private equity firm first buys it.

We've observed a multiple expansion effect when private equity funds are used to buy good companies and make them even better. You tend to achieve a higher multiple when selling a better company. These factors in combination are powerful drivers of private equity returns.

Bob: What steps does a PEG take to make good companies even better?

Rob: During the hold period, after they've made the decision to buy at a certain price, our best private equity funds augment and build up the existing management teams of the companies. While the output is increased cash flow, the mechanism is a better management team. The best PEGs have access to superior talent and put them to work in these companies, so it's completely rational why this occurs.

A company might grow to a level under the original owner, but entrepreneurs have different risk profiles and different issues that make them tick. They make decisions for their own reasons, some of which might not align with profit maximization of the firm. While entrepreneurs might earn a lot of money, they also make some decisions that don't build maximum long-term value.

PEGs also employ better accounting systems and are more precise in their use of accounting information. Entrepreneurially managed companies are probably staffed by someone who is best described as a controller, whereas the private equity funds hire someone described as a CFO: someone who is able to think strategically, get behind the numbers, and make better decisions firm-wide.

Third, if you look at how the entrepreneurs approach their financial statements, in many cases they'll ask, "What's the minimum I have to spend to get these things done?" If they are contemplating a sale, paying more for audited statements for the three years before they make a transaction would be extremely beneficial.

Bob: Why are audited financial statements important? How do they add value?

Rob: The owner needs to consider how an outsider would view the company. Outsiders realize that the entrepreneur knows everything about his business, because he's lived with it. But outsiders don't have that comfort level, and so they need high quality information. How do you quickly and accurately fulfill that need? By handing outsiders audited statements. That reduces some variance around the transaction.

Not all entrepreneurs are risk takers, but they are able to tolerate risk differently than the rest of us. PEGs operate on a different risk level than your typical entrepreneur. For example, an entrepreneur might look at a new customer account with which they already have 30 percent customer concentration. If they take it up to 35 percent or 40 percent, they could make an extra million dollars. Conversely, PEGs might say, "You're driving up your customer concentration." They are thinking about how to position the company for closing, and they don't want to sell a company with 40 percent customer concentration.

Bob: What are some other accounting issues?

Rob: Internally, practice better cost accounting to determine the real costs of products or services. Often, the entrepreneur will view their bottom line and say, "The company is making $20 million in revenue and $2 million in profit. I'm making big money. No need to push harder." In fact, they might find that 20 percent or 30 percent of their products are driving profitability, and the rest are just driving revenue. PEGs examine such issues.

Bob: PEGs understand the value of capital. Can you expand on that?

Rob: Yes, PEGs have a good handle on the value of capital, and I'm not sure if an entrepreneur has a firm grasp on that. An entrepreneur might say, "I want to build this company, and I've got a million dollars to invest in a plant and equipment." PEGs might ask, "Why build a plant?" The entrepreneur could respond, "So I don't have to pay rent." PEGs might say, "We don't want to be in the real estate business."

Bob: Any other beneficial practices you typically see?

Rob: PEGs are keen on establishing a solid management team, installing accounting controls, and occasionally beefing up the IT system. Applying a prudent amount of leverage on the company is most vital. PEGs are better at establishing a capital structure that has the proper mix of debt and equity.

Bob: Most of your earnings come from the sale of portfolio companies. How and when do you decide to sell a company?

Rob: As a fund to funds, we generally don't make that decision. The best PEGs sell a company when they have a compelling reason. A company might have evolved to where it's "outgrown" the fund, and it's time for a larger PEG to take over. Maybe the company does need to add a $20 million plant, and they've out-grown the PEG.

PEGs want to ensure that their capital is compounding at a rate that exceeds their internal rate-of-return thresholds. If the company is not compounding at that rate, PEGs will be leery of holding onto that company.

PEGs sell while there's still meat on the bone, something tangible for the next buyer. Chances are, that buyer will be even more sophisticated than the last buyer was.

Bob: So, you want to sell a company when it's growing and has opportunities for significant additional earnings, because that's when it's most attractive. If you keep it for too long, you'll miss the increment associated with the increase in the value of the entity.

Rob: Yes, the three ways to make money from a leveraged buyout are paying down debt, increasing the cash flow, and increasing the multiple. PEGs make a trade-off. They attain a higher multiple on an existing cash flow if tangible growth is likely, instead of waiting for a higher cash flow and a lower multiple sometime in the future. We've seen PEGs sell for phenomenal multiples—sometimes even up to fifteen times EBITDA—because they've demonstrated a clear growth path ahead.

Bob: We often look at the trailing twelve months to evaluating what the multiple was when it sold.

Rob: The larger the company, the more intangible the valuation can become—in an IPO market, you might have negative cash flow or breakeven cash flow, but you can see a clear path to $50 million of EBITDA. The multiple today might be meaningless, but the multiple for next year's EBITDA might be enticing.

It all depends on the company's positioning and prospects. Most of our companies are not IPO. They are in the $5 to $25 million EBITDA range, with positive cash flows and traditional industry multiples.

In 2009, we saw a lot of companies experience a U-type of growth: they took a tremendous pounding but started to come back in 2010. You could not sell the 2010 promise using the 2009 performance. You might be able to sell the 2011 or 2012 promise, however, off the 2010 performance.

Bob: Expert management is vital...

Rob: Yes. When we invest with PEGs, we know that can find the best CEOs to head their acquired companies. Such CEOs are the mechanism to achieving better earnings and giving us the desired rate of return. Also, a solid board of directors composed of other people from the industry can add significant value to a company. An experienced board gives the CEO the ability to bounce ideas around and not sit on top of the mountain by him or herself, which is what most entrepreneurs do.

GOING TO MARKET: FINDING A BUYER

When you are looking for a buyer for your business, potential acquirers will come in one of several stripes: synergistic buyers, employee-owned stock option plans (ESOPs), family members, merger partners, or investors such as PEGs. Each brings different benefits and drawbacks.

Synergistic buyers. Synergistic buyers are generally industry players that would want your business either to integrate horizontally (i.e., your business represents an opportunity to increase the products or services it offers, its customer base, or its geographic reach) or vertically (i.e., it represents an opportunity to take more control of the development, manufacturing, marketing, or distribution process).

Synergistic buyers can be good acquirers because they will generally understand the specific benefits of buying your company. They will also, however, have a good understanding of the risks associated with your industry and thus have a disposition to underbid. Not being professional buyers, they may have an incomplete understanding of your business's true value, and you can chew up a lot of time and energy attempting to sell to someone who was more or less destined to offer you an inadequate price.

In addition, such buyers are often your current direct competition. During the due diligence phase of the transaction, you will have to reveal a great deal of confidential information. If for some reason the transaction falls through, you will incur a fair degree of exposure and vulnerability. When we serve as intermediaries in synergistic transactions, we try to reveal as little confidential information as possible during the transaction process. Nevertheless, potential buyers must have access to a fairly complete range of information in order to make a decision. This is a process that must be carefully navigated.

ESOPs. An employee stock ownership program (ESOP) represents another alternative. Often, you can receive a full valuation in establishing an ESOP, enjoy some tax benefits, and gain some other advantages, as well. ESOPs, however, are fraught with land mines. To finance the transaction, the owner often has to preside as a guarantor to the loan for employees to buy the company. This can prove risky.

Family members. Selling or transferring your business to your children or relatives can be as complex as selling to strangers. If family members wish to manage the business, you can 1) sell to them outright, 2) transfer the company to them while you're alive, or 3) transfer the company upon your death. For transfers, you'll need a succession plan that specifies how the business will operate once

101

you're gone. This reduces the potential for squabbles while helping to ensure effective continuity.

Merger partners. If an outright, lucrative sale of your business is not on the horizon, you may find that valid reasons exist for merging with another company. These could include the ability to combine both companies' capital or, even better, to combine the various components of each company, which together are worth more than the sum of their parts.

PEGs. After reading for several chapters about the expertise and success of PEGs, you might be intrigued about being acquired by one. There are many good reasons to sell to a PEG (although you will only have the opportunity if your business meets a PEG's often-stringent investment criteria).

- **Capital growth.** We know that PEGs are not afraid to borrow money or to invest money to take advantage of appropriate opportunities. By contrast, business owners, even highly creative and innovative types, often fail to exploit their own ideas. When business owners sell to PEGs, several phenomena occur, one of which is that owners are incentivized to do what they do best: make their ideas come alive.

- **The Good Housekeeping Seal of Approval.** Some argue that as soon as a company is owned by a PEG, its value increases because the company's management is more focused and disciplined. Also, the risk to a future buyer is seen as lower than when that same potential buyer deals directly with the private business owner. In fact, the day a PEG acquires a business, that business is valued more highly in the eyes of larger buyers. This is true even if there are no changes to the business whatsoever. A PEG's acquisition is like a "Good Housekeeping Seal of Approval." Thereafter, the measures that the PEG applies on a consistent and disciplined basis enable it to demand a higher price for that business from the next acquirer.

- **Experts.** Of the many benefits PEGs bring to the table, one of the most important is their extensive roster of contacts. A PEG's contacts invariably contain experts in IT, logistics, marketing, search engine optimization, and a variety of other areas. The best PEGs know the right experts for nearly every potential situation, and these key people generally prove to be ultra-important. For example, a client of ours produces a sophisticated software program that offers users a new level of security and defense. The PEG studying this company and considering its acquisition retained the services of a sophisticated marketing firm, which confirmed the entrepreneur's sales potential claims with several Asian and far-Eastern governments. This is only one example of many indicating the level of expertise upon which PEGs can draw. Such expertise ultimately benefits businesses and rewards business owners in ways that they simply would not experience otherwise.

- **Due diligence and then some.** Unbeknownst to most middle-market business owners, before a PEG closes on a transaction, it undertakes an incredible amount of due diligence (See Appendix B, Due Diligence). This is necessary because PEGs have a fiduciary responsibility to their investors.

  With one of our clients representing a $60 million pending transaction, the PEG invested $400,000 in a variety of due diligence activities, including marketing research, financial analysis, and travel to specific sites. Moreover, it's not unusual for a PEG to invest between $500,000 and $2.5 million in due diligence activities when considering acquisitions in the $5 million to $40 million range.

  When a PEG spends $500,000 or more in due diligence activities, sometimes they determine that a potential acquisition is not worth pursuing. This happens more often than you might presume. There are many reasons to acquire a business but many more not to acquire it. It's not unusual to hear of PEGs that consider a hundred businesses or more before choosing one to acquire. The business owner who realizes the value of being acquired will be subjected to a systematic examination of internal and external factors affecting the business's past, current, and future before a closing will occur.

- **The slingshot effect.** If a PEG expresses interest in your business, it could already have strategies for increasing your company's revenue to pursue immediately after acquiring it. In some cases, PEGs have customers or clients, channels of distribution, or other sales targets already lined up and will tap them quickly. The potential to increase revenue upon acquisition puts the company on an accelerated path to higher valuation. Any minority share you retain is likely to rise accordingly. The beauty of benefitting from other people's contacts is that a wide range of new customers/ clients previously untapped might now become repeat or long-term customers—on top of the long-term customers that you've retained. Adding to the customer base by 10 percent to 30 percent or more creates substantial incremental revenue with an outsized effect on pretax net profit (as overhead has already been fully covered).

- **Keeping some skin in the game.** Another reason to be acquired by a PEG is the ability to enjoy a second bite of the apple after you sell, provided you retain some equity in the transaction. PEGs have no interest in becoming the day-to-day managers of the business and would typically like you to stay on. Many business owners have not considered that by staying on with the business in a minority ownership position, they could realize their dreams in ways that were not available before.

Using someone else's capital, owners can approach the business again with new eyes and a new perspective, almost like a second life. Our experience reveals that most business owners are not ready or willing to retire, even after selling their businesses. They have years of productive life in front of them. By staying on with the business, they get to be productive in ways for which they previously did not have time.

We often hear owners and managers saying, "We want to take this business to the next level." So they're aware of significant growth opportunities, but they have never precisely defined them, don't know how to approach them, or haven't been willing to invest the money and incur the risks to exploit higher-level opportunities. They become intrigued by the idea of selling the business to a PEG when they realize they're going to attain the management expertise and capital that makes reaching higher levels possible. And here's the bonus: business owners can often eventually sell their retained equity at a greater value than the majority interest originally sold.

With a PEG as a partner, business owners are more likely to have better results than going it alone. Thus, owners achieve the best of both worlds by selling to a PEG. They can take some of their own chips off the table, benefit from financial diversification of their personal balance sheet, and continue to own an interest in the company they founded as it progresses toward a higher valuation.

From a personal and social perspective, owners who sell to PEGs can maintain their standing in the community and can accept board and advisory board positions with other companies, unlike when they ran their own enterprise. They can serve the community, volunteer, and even travel.

One entrepreneur we worked with—owner of a recycling business—created his own "slingshot effect" by retaining equity in a sale to a PEG. In the transaction, the owner kept a 30 percent share of the equity and stayed to provide management services—in particular, for a specific division of the recycling enterprise that proved to be highly profitable. As it turned out, the PEG hadn't focused on this division at all. The owner made a deal with the PEG to cross-fertilize operations and earned himself far more money annually than he had been making from the entire company when he had fully owned it. With his retained equity and stock purchase rights, his 30 percent equity rose from under a $1 million annually to $5 million by 2011, with a projected $40 million four years hence.

Typically, owners who stay on retain equity in a range between 10 percent and 30 percent of their company. At that level of ownership, PEGs believe that the owner will continue to have a vested interest in how the company fares. PEGs also want owners to retain equity because in the case where they buy only 75 percent of the company, they can employ 100 percent of the assets in the business to make the acquisition and to fund repayment of the acquisition leverage, as well as its cash flow.

Several reasons exist for maintaining equity in your business. Realistically, you have to do something with your money. Considering all the potential financial sinkholes you can encounter when investing, maintaining an investment in the business that you founded—which is now being expertly managed and financed by top-level professionals—represents a sound and viable investment strategy.

PEGs do not invest in businesses that they believe are going to fail or maintain flat earnings. They invest in ventures that they think will become spectacular successes in achieving a high multiple upon selling it. You want to be along for that ride.

Maintaining an equity share of your business makes sense as well because it's likely that you know nothing better in this world than the company's opportunities and risks. Thus, you are in a prime position to be a valuable source of insight and wisdom, which, in partnership with the PEG, will keep the business's prospects on an upward trajectory. The opportunity to gain the same advantages as the PEG is compelling.

When the sale of your business is handled effectively and you maintain an equity interest within it, the return on the tangible and intangible assets represent a better investment opportunity with higher returns than they ever could prior to the sale of the company. Also, when a previous business owner enthusiastically wants to retain equity as well as participation in the company, PEGs as well as future buyers conclude, "This owner believes in the future of the business. Here is a viable partner."

Conversely, owners who want to cash out completely and retain no equity send the wrong signal to buyers, who conclude that the owner wants to cut and run. That makes them concerned about what aspects of the business might not be so evident.

PEG PURCHASE CRITERIA

It's important to understand the transaction from a PEG's perspective and to keep in mind that while they're evaluating your business, they're evaluating many others as well. If they make the decision to acquire your business, that decision comes at a time when they're deciding on other businesses as well.

Internal rate of return. Chart 4, "Widget Manufacturing Company Internal Rate of Return Analysis," shows side-by-side comparisons of two different computations for internal rate of return. The first example shows an internal rate of return of 27.78 percent over five to seven years. Where on earth can you get that kind of return? Hardly anywhere.

PEGs consistently achieve these kinds of returns, on average, across a variety of businesses in which they've invested. Out of any ten acquisitions, PEGs might enjoy a couple of grand slams. Most companies perform as expected, while a few go into the tank, offering no return whatsoever.

How are PEGs able to succeed? Keep in mind that the investments they make are not liquid. It takes a long time to sell a privately held company: anywhere from six to eighteen months, with the average being about a year. So, PEGs invest a lot of time and energy when acquiring a business. They never rush into it. Once they decide acquire a business, they'll put all the management skill into that firm that they deem necessary.

Chart 4

Widget Mfg. Co., Inc.
Internal Rate of Return Analysis: Computation 1

		Year	Investment and/or Residual	Annual Debt Payments	Annual EBITDA	35% Tax on Net Inc after IDA	Capex	Annual After Tax Cash Flow
EBITDA	964,000	0	($1,928,000)	$0	$0	$0	$0	($1,928,000)
Deal Factor	4	1	$0	($333,197)	$964,000	($249,900)	($100,000)	$280,903
Deal Value	$3,856,000	2	$0	($333,197)	$1,012,200	($266,770)	($100,000)	$312,233
Debt Factor	50.00%	3	$0	($333,197)	$1,062,810	($284,484)	($100,000)	$345,130
Annual Capex	($100,000)	4	$0	($333,197)	$1,115,951	($303,083)	($100,000)	$379,761
EBITDA Growth	5%/year	5	$0	($333,197)	$1,171,748	($322,612)	($100,000)	$415,939
Discount Rate	5.00%	6	$0	($333,197)	$1,230,335	($343,117)	($100,000)	$454,021
IRR	27.78%	7	$4,979,897	($333,197)	$1,291,852	($364,648)	($100,000)	$5,494,704
Debt/Equity	50.00%							
Total Debt	$1,928,000	Totals	$3,042,557	($2,332,379)	$7,848,836			$5,724,691
Total Equity	$1,928,000							
Loan Amort Rate	5.00%							
Loan Amort Years	7.00%							

IDA = Interest, Depreciation, and Amortization = $250,000/year

Bob, the end of the r.h. column on this one was cut off – need the rest of the numbers

Widget Mfg. Co., Inc.
Internal Rate of Return Analysis: Computation 2

		Year	Investment and/or Residual	Annual Debt Payments	Annual EBITDA	35% Tax on Net Inc after IDA	Capex	Annual After Tax Cash Flow
EBITDA	964,000	0	($2,410,000)	$0	$0	$0	$0	($2,410)
Deal Factor	5	1	$0	($416,496)	$964,000	($249,900)	($100,000)	$197
Deal Value	$4,820,000	2	$0	($416,496)	$1,012,200	($266,770)	($100,000)	$228
Debt Factor	50.00%	3	$0	($416,496)	$1,062,810	($284,484)	($100,000)	$261
Annual Capex	($100,000)	4	$0	($416,496)	$1,115,951	($303,083)	($100,000)	$296
EBITDA Growth	5%/year	5	$0	($416,496)	$1,171,748	($322,612)	($100,000)	$332
Discount Rate	5.00%	6	$0	($416,496)	$1,230,335	($343,117)	($100,000)	$370
IRR	22.57%	7	$6,213,372	($416,496)	$1,291,852	($364,648)	($100,000)	$6,624
Debt/Equity	50.00%							
Total Debt	$2,410,000	Totals	$3,803,372	($2,915,472)	$7,848,836			$6,342
Total Equity	$2,410,000							
Loan Amort Rate	5.00%							
Loan Amort Years	7.00%							

IDA = Interest, Depreciation, and Amortization = $250,000/year

In Chart 4, the 27.78 percent internal rate of return in the first analysis is acceptable to PEGs, and thus, they would invest in the business. The second analysis, which assumes a higher level of debt, results in a 22.57 percent internal rate of return, which falls below the 25 percent threshold that PEGs seek.

If they believe that the company's performance is better reflected in the second analysis, PEGs would not acquire the company. Said another way, if the company's selling price is $3.8 million, PEGs can make a go of it. If the selling price is $4.8 million, PEGs will not take the risk. Understandably, a business owner would want to sell for $4.8 million rather than $3.8 million if given the chance. As in all business transactions, if the price of an item is too high, it may not sell at all.

As the business owner, if you understand that a PEG's threshold is 25 percent and that it will not acquire for a lesser internal rate of return, that can influence your selling. Perhaps you'll lower your price to $4.2 million from $4.8 million, which translates into an attractive projected return for PEGs. Or you might acquire a smaller company that offers a good, service, or capability that complements those of your existing company. As a result of that acquisition, the numbers might work for the PEG. You might be able to spin off an element of your business that is underperforming. Either strategy is bold but could be prudent based on your financial positioning.

Purchase analysis. Chart 5, "Widget Manufacturing Purchase Analysis," sheds light on the value and associated costs of operating (and eventually selling) a business. This analysis is like shorthand. It indicates on one page the owner's financial position upon sale, with all the smoke and mirrors extracted.

After considering the assets and liabilities that an owner will retain upon sale, the cash the owner will receive, and the associated closing expenses, the resulting tax allocations are revealed. These allocations show the owner's and shareholders' after-tax benefits.

The three columns on the top of the page, including "Assets Purchased," "Transaction Structure," and "Tax Allocation," show the business owner what is being sold, the tax implications, and what the owner will be receiving. At the subheading "Cash at Closing Estimate," the last item, "Total After-Tax Benefit to Shareholders," equals $3,880,143. Such calculations are crucial because they show the business owner's precise dollar takeaway at closing: exactly where the owner will stand financially.

PEGs routinely undertake such analysis. Some business owners or their financial advisers do so, as well. Many business owners, however, cannot and do not undertake such analysis. Thus, working with an intermediary before selling to a PEG is vital.

Chart 5

Widget Mfg. Co., Inc.
Purchase Analysis
$964,000 EBITDA, Purchase Price 4.5x + $4,338,000

	Assets Purchased	Transaction Structure	Tax Allocation
Assets			
Fixed Assets	$1,788,350		$1,788,350
Accumulated Depreciation	($1,244,086)		($1,244,086)
Net Book Valued Fixed Assets	$544,264		$544,264
Accounts Receivable	$568,312		$568,312
Inventory	$584,488		$584,488
Total Tangible Assets per Books	$1,697,064		$1,697,064
Intangible/Goodwill Value	$2,893,742		$2,893,742
Total Consideration	$4,590,806		
Cash at Closing (for Business)		$4,338,000	
Current Liabilities Assumed (A/P + Accrued Expense)		$252,806	
Total Consideration		$4,590,806	
Total Allocated for Tax Purposes			$4,590,806
Calculation of Estimated Taxes			
Pre-tax Profit (100% allocated to Goodwill)	$2,893,742		
Less Estimated Closing Expenses	($250,000)		
Estimate of Pre-tax Gain on Goodwill	$264,372		
Assume Cap Gain Rate of 15%	($396,561)		
Total Federal Taxes Payable	$396,561		
Cash at Closing Estimate			
Consideration at Closing	$4,338,000		
Less Closing Expenses	($250,000)		
Less Estimate Taxes (R.E. + Business Gain)	($396,561)		
Plus Retained Cash & Investments	$268,704		
Total Estimated Cash at Closing + Retained Assets	$3,960,143		
Liabilities Retained	($80,000)		
Total Cash at Closing	$3,880,143		

TERMS OF THE DEAL

The major elements of any deal include the purchase price, how it is determined, and how the funds will be paid; terms and conditions of employment for the owner and key management; noncompete provisions; conditions to closing; tax allocations; contingencies for financing; validation of major contracts; and other potential contingencies associated with a major transaction. Both you and the acquirer will want to structure the deal to minimize downstream risk as far as possible.

If the price is nice. The total purchase price that a bidder is willing to pay for a business often is the key issue in the owner's acceptance of a deal; depending on other terms, though, it might not prove to be so critical. Our clients sometimes have chosen a lesser price because they liked the acquiring people better than others, terms were more favorable, or they saw other advantages. Cash in the owner's pocket and the owner's percentage of retained equity after the sale are certainly major considerations.

A successful sale will include both a detailed analysis of net worth and capital and a target value for the company at the closing. This value impacts the final purchase price, dollar for dollar, right up to the minute that the agreement is consummated.

When deciding to acquire a company, the buyer either purchases the firm's assets or its stock. Asset purchases include acquiring a company's plant and facilities, equipment, inventory, vehicles, etc. Stock purchases include only acquiring the company's stock. Either case poses significant advantages and disadvantages.

Assets and liabilities. These—and how they are included in the transaction—are significant deal terms. For an acquisition to proceed, a specific list of the assets and liabilities to be included in the sale, as well as excluded (in other words, retained by the owner), must be drawn up in advance and agreed to by all parties. Any

111

personal assets the owner seeks to retain need to be identified. The exact amount of net working capital included in the purchase price must be specified, as well as the method for determining how the price is adjusted for variations at closing.

Employee agreements. In addition, acquirers need to know about any employee agreements that are in force, including terms related to duration, benefits, compensation, and perquisites, as well as associated responsibilities and any applicable bonuses or earn-outs that may be forthcoming to employees. The owner will be asked to sign a non-compete clause or a non-circumvention clause, which specifies the duration, range, or radius, and specific activities that he or she may engage in following the sale of the company. (Note: Key employees will probably also be asked to sign non-compete/non-circumvention agreements.) No PEG wants to take the reigns of a business only to find that the previous owner has set up next door and represents major competition.

Taxes. Taxes and how they are handled play an important role in the terms of a deal. Tax allocation is critical in maximizing the after-tax net associated with the sale of a business. The business owner invariably seeks to maximize allocation to goodwill, to maximize his or her reward for devoting years to building the business's reputation. Both federal and state taxes need to be accounted for, as well as licenses, transfer fees, sales taxes, and any applicable local taxes. All such taxes and fees represent potential land mines in regard to a successful acquisition, and they need to be delineated in the sales agreement.

Management after closing. After the closing, matters related to management represent potential land mines. Who will be the day-to-day manager? Who will sit on the company's board? Will the PEG charge the company for management services? Management arrangements can vary widely, usually based on the level of services provided. Sometimes, a fee is paid to PEG management at closing so that they can begin anew with a cash flow injection.

Other. Representations and warranties must be appropriately limited to minimize the seller's downstream risk. If you are going to be a partner in the deal, how will the balance sheet appear immediately after the closing? Will your retained equity be treated as part of the PEG's investment? If so, this needs to be agreed upon in advance. If a seller's note is involved, how exactly will it be structured? Who is first in the pecking order, and how might the note impact the debt-equity structure of the business after closing? Will there be any cash distributions to you so that you're able to cover any tax liabilities as a result of the sale? How will the proceeds from the sale be divided?

THE NEGOTIATION

Because much can go wrong in the process leading up to a sale, it's vital for both parties to negotiate with precision. For example, in determining the net working capital to be conveyed, specify an agreed-upon third-party accountant who will audit the inventory, receivables, and payables shortly after closing, so that even if a specific amount has been stipulated, appropriate adjustments can be made to the final purchase price of the business.

In the following chapter, I will delve more deeply into how you can protect yourself when negotiating a sale.

ONE TASK AT A TIME

If you're now feeling a bit overwhelmed, take heart. You're likely underprepared to entertain a great offer for your business if it comes in the next few days or weeks. However, this month you can take action on a couple ideas that you've gleaned from this book. Even if you're deficient in many areas, get started in one or two key areas right now. You'll be far better off than if you don't start at all. Most owners prefer to tackle a combination of tasks. Thus, if they can't proceed on one of them on any given day, they can make headway on another.

Taking on too much at once is frustrating and self-defeating, so avoid biting off more than you can chew. You're better off achieving a few short-term wins that help you to bolster your longer-term campaign, maximize the value of your business, and sell it for a good multiple.

SHORT-TERM GAINS, LONG-TERM WINS

A college buddy of mine landed a job with Burroughs, which ultimately became Unisys, a hardware manufacturer that competed directly with IBM for the manufacture and sale of banking industry technology. He told me that the Burroughs sales training program focused on ensuring that trainees would be able to use and demonstrate the equipment that the company sold to businesses.

Recognizing that new hires might go months and months before actually selling a product and receiving a commission, Burroughs also trained new hires on how to use and sell a relatively inexpensive line of calculators. The theory was that on the way to selling equipment in the $20,000 range, when the trainees had the opportunity to make sales in the $200 to $500 range, they would be experiencing small victories. The human psyche, theoretically, doesn't know the difference between a big win and a small win. The subconscious mind, it is presumed, takes in everything and rates common occurrences as wins or losses.

By having a series of little wins along the way, new hires avoided experiencing complete dry spells with zero opportunity to pull out a sales contract and write up a sale. The ability to sell *something* and to put your name on the big sales board at the office, whether your sales were small or not, seemed much better than having a zero next to your name week after week and month after month. So it is with business owners who are preparing their businesses for sale.

You have dozens of issues to handle, and you can't get to them all at once. Action, however, is invigorating. Several small actions can add up to a large one. Even action with less-than-desirable results, one can argue, is more invigorating than immobility. When you focus on items that need attention, give yourself a sufficient time horizon, and you'll feel better about the large task of preparing your business for sale.

INTERVIEW: THE FINE POINTS OF DEAL TERMS

Gary Humphreys is an entrepreneur with some keen insights on the fine points of deal terms, as this interview reveals.

Bob: Can you offer a brief background of Able Tire and your ownership of it?

Gary: We started Able Tire in 1992 with $5,000 cash, a used pickup, and a trailer. I cut a deal to haul scrap tires for recyclers for twenty-five cents a tire and did it by myself. We grew steadily from one truck and one employee, usually only borrowing for hard assets like another truck and never borrowing for expansion or capital improvements.

When we reached a couple million dollars in annual revenue, and we weren't worrying if we could make payroll, we expanded beyond Dallas-Fort Worth into the Houston market. Growth was rapid, so we expanded to the San Antonio-Austin market, and soon we had an 85 percent market share in three-quarters of the state and about a 65 percent market share in the whole state of Texas. We continued to grow and were more aggressive in offering value-added products. We were able to increase market share in a sustainable way.

In 2007, we decided to sell a portion of the company to take some chips off the table. We hired you and your firm to help us cross the ultimate finish line, and in May of 2008, we closed a deal with Liberty Tire.

Bob: What was your driving motivation to sell?

Gary: To be a competitor outside the regional market, I needed to spend some capital—minimum of $10 to $20 million dollars. It became more advantageous for me to sell a percentage of my company and help someone else expand nationally using their capital. I didn't have to guarantee any notes!

Bob: Why grow the company at all? Why couldn't you have remained static?

Gary: In hindsight, I probably could have, and I would have been fine. But in '06 and '07, there were some major pushes to consolidate. Liberty Tire was a huge player, and they were aggressive, backed by private equity money. To compete, smaller players were combining too many operations into one. I decided to take a leap and expand in a big way; that's why I chose Liberty.

Bob: Many business owners wonder whether to continue growing the company, sell out partially or fully, or consolidate with another smaller player. You waited, but then you decided it was in your best interest to sell to the largest consolidator.

Gary: Another PEG that I had liked was concerned about our market share and our high concentration with customers. Approximately 50 percent of our business was with one customer, and that was an issue for the PEG. Liberty, however, saw that as a big plus because they had been desperate to win that customer. So, for Liberty, the deal was worth a premium; for the PEG, acquiring us was problematic.

Bob: Was there any action that you should or should not have taken concerning Liberty?

Gary: Ultimately, I'd do it again today. We got a fair price, and I was happy with the earn-out. Liberty was probably unhappy with some of the earn-out because it far exceeded their ideal payout. Negotiations turned out much better than we had anticipated, but worse than they had anticipated.

Bob: With the excellent earn-out you negotiated, did you make more money with Liberty than you would have if you had continued to own Able outright?

Gary: Yes, and not just the earn-out. If you look at my annual income for Able Tire pre-closing, it was around $100,000 a month. Since I closed, I negotiated the leases on all the properties back to me for five years, triple net. I got a great earn-out, and I negotiated a great salary, car allowance, and insurance coverage. So now, my monthly income is closer to $130,000. Essentially, I gained $30,000 a month and became free of all the notes.

Bob: When negotiating an earn-out, what's your advice for maximize the post-closing reward?

Gary: You have to be specific about the earn-out and have measurable goals. You've got to leave valuation and subjectivity out of the picture. If the agreed-upon goal is increasing revenue by 10 percent, understand the applicable baseline and have that agreed upon by both companies. If it's to decrease expenses by 10 percent, then have the baseline of expenses and what is included in that discount.

If you anticipate an argument about which items affect the bottom line, they need to be spelled out. If EBITDA is employed, a corporate overhead that you might not understand will be added. You have to remove all ambiguity about the figures.

Bob: Did you overlook anything or make any errors during the earn-out? Did anything surprise you?

Gary: I left chips on the table on the increased EBITDA budget. We had put a combined budget together for the first year of $5.3 million. If I made the $5.3 million budget from May to May, then I got $1.4 million, half in stock and half in cash. In retrospect, I wish I could have put it on a scale, so that if I made 80 percent of the budget, I got 80 percent, but if I exceeded it, I made 150 percent. After the first year, I made $6.1 million. I beat the target by $800,000.

Bob: So, allow for possibilities on both the downside and the upside: bonuses on the upside and still some kind of benefit for a shortfall.

Gary: Sure, understanding full well that on the other side of the table, they are going to have limitations. Eighty percent of any earn-out would be acceptable; anything less than 80 percent is not.

Bob: As a component of your transaction, you negotiated for shares in the acquiring company. Why? It turned out to be beneficial. How do you see the opportunities?

Gary: I did it because we were going to take the company from a $25 million EBITDA to a budgeted $60 million EBITDA this year. The larger the EBITDA becomes, the larger the multiple will be, so I knew that I would make money on my stock. It was risk-reward. I knew the upside for me was worth going with the stock. If somebody is unsure, my suggestion would be to take more cash and less stock.

Bob: Did you also have the option to buy more shares with your own cash?

Gary: I did, and I bought the maximum amount I could. I thought that the company was going in the right direction, making substantial growth in revenue and EBITDA, and that the payday was worth it. I kept 30 percent of the original transaction in stock, rolled over tax-free.

Bob: Because of your role in Liberty, you basically have been on both sides of the table. You've been a business owner in a private company, and now you are a principal in a portfolio company owned by a PEG. How does American Securities handle a company like Liberty? What do they hope to accomplish?

Gary: They hope to sell it for a lot more money than they bought it for. That's the philosophy in running the company. We have the same philosophy as a management group. We want to increase revenue and EBITDA, provide stable line items, and make the business attractive, so that the next buyer wants to pay more for it. We install consistent and stable practices.

Suppose that instead of thirty-nine independent restaurants, we're going to become thirty-nine McDonald's franchises. We aren't close from a production standpoint, but we are close from an administrative, accounting, and logistics standpoint. From a sales and marketing standpoint, we're making major strides. Rolling stock is becoming more consistent, and our equipment purchases are becoming more consistent.

If we're weak in one area, it is our production or manufacturing plants. That will take a sizeable capital infusion. We think that if all the other components are in place, then that's a benefit the next acquirer can enjoy.

Bob: What's the economic reward in having consistency throughout the divisions?

Gary: Ease of management. You wouldn't have to pay for the big guns or the specialized guys. You wouldn't need a "Gary" anymore, because you would know how the trucks operate up and down the road, how the machine turns on, and how the product moves from one side of the building to the other. Those are all consistent practices that can be taught, implemented, and standardized.

Bob: Why is it easier to do this in a larger environment under a PEG than as an individual owner?

Gary: …I think it's harder, but the individual owner never has the foresight or enthusiasm to do it. He thinks, "Work is pretty good. Every year we have sustainable growth and profit. Our safety records are pretty good." So, he's either going to go build houses or go play golf, and he's not going to concentrate on that other stuff so much.

Bob: Is American Securities all about maximizing their exit strategy? If so, what do they do on a daily basis to be prepared to sell at any time?

Gary: They stay on top of information associated with the company, with financial metrics and audits. If someone comes into town potentially to buy the company, we can easily show him production data, fuel usage, capital equipment lists, and financials.

Bob: So, database management is imperative. You have to know how they are handling their customers, suppliers, employees, production, and all the other elements of their business. That way, you know exactly what they are doing at any time. They basically manage their business by the numbers.

Gary: You're only as good as the last thirty days in this business, but it's hard to sustain morale and keep good managers when everyone is hammered on the numbers. After a while, people burn out on that stuff, and that's a little bit frustrating. For me, however, the numbers are vital, and I know when it's a payday, so I'm happy.

Bob: If business owners seek to maximize their overall outcome, how should they transition from the initial closing to the period where they are working for someone else?

Gary: The philosophy is, look: you are getting married to the buyer. You need to know who they are, what their philosophy is, and who their key managers are. If you can't fall in love with them, it's going to be hard to do business with them post-closing.

We do have acquisitions in which the owners don't work out. We have to get them out of the deal, because they're not taking the direction we want the company to take. They're set in their ways, and they don't want to change.

That wasn't the case with me. When I realized that I could work with these guys and have a good relationship, it was easier to negotiate all the pieces of the pie.

Bob: You are personable, but many owners are not; they're introverted. How does someone like that develop a personal touch, and why is it so important?

Gary: I don't think you're going to change people. I think you need to decide as a team how to use that personality to get the most production. It could be in a role where he doesn't have to communicate with customers, but he's still producing for the company. You've got to let them succeed in that role without removing them from their comfort zone. And you need to address the issue right off the bat.

Bob: Are there any significant differences between how PEGs and private business owners manage a company?

Gary: As we've covered from a numbers standpoint, it's completely different. PEGs look at EBITDA and balance sheet line items, whereas owners expense everything and minimize their tax exposure. From a philosophical standpoint, there are many similarities. Running a business isn't brain surgery. You want a safe environment, productive employees, and overall efficiency.

Bob: In terms of taking some chips off the table and still keeping an interest in the company, where has this relationship met your expectations, and where have there been surprises?

Gary: It's met 100 percent of my objectives because our region and our company met budgeted projections, and the management group proved to be just like they were when we were "dating." When we got "married," they were the same people.

Bob: Any other observations?

Gary: If you have an interest in selling, you need to plow forward and be committed. Otherwise, you're going to waste a lot of time, and sometimes you'll burn relationships that you'll wish you hadn't.

Bob: So while it was a difficult experience, you stayed with it because you were committed to it, and it turned out to be worthwhile?

Gary: Yes. It was especially difficult when we first thought we had a deal and the group withdrew. That was a real gut punch. To get back up and move forward with commitment is like re-mounting the horse that threw you: you've got to get back on and proceed.

Bob: You went from an outsider to an insider in the private equity world and the investment world. Because of that, you are able to evaluate significant and lucrative investment opportunities that otherwise would have been alien to you. I think that's something we don't stress enough, that there are ancillary benefits to being acquired that you can't even imagine when you take the first bite of the apple.

Gary: Absolutely.

Chapter 6: Protecting Yourself and Everything You've Earned

You're only going to sell your business once. And for all the benefits I've discussed about selling to an interested acquirer, especially a PEG, you nevertheless must be wary when entering into a deal. Buyers are not looking out for you; they are looking out for themselves. PEGs in particular are masters at maximizing their returns—so you need to be a master as well, or hire a master to assist you.

In this chapter, I'll discuss a couple of major areas to look out for in protecting your interests before and during a purchase deal. And then I'll provide some more examples of how qualified intermediaries are vital in helping you achieve your goal of obtaining maximum value from your business.

Protect Your Assets

As we saw in Chapter 1's readiness matrix, a business has to be in the ready state to sell, and the owner has to have the right mindset to sell. Prior to closing, part of an owner's responsibility is understanding his or her financial requirements so that he or she can protect the net worth the business has generated, provide for the family, and have a life.

For example, minimizing the tax burden from your sale is crucial. Current US tax code requires that citizens pay taxes on worldwide income, derived both here and abroad. Even individuals with international asset protection trusts are liable and responsible to pay taxes on that trust, and any associated income, to the US Internal Revenue Service. We believe that once a business owner cashes in, an asset protection trust is a necessity. There are simply too many risks not to implement this "insurance," which protects your assets from the claims of third parties.

As homeowners, we know that it makes sense to have sufficient levels of property and casualty insurance, and we wouldn't drive our cars without adequate auto insurance. We wouldn't hand over our keys to a teenager who is irresponsible, yet horror stories abound about adults who've done so.

Likewise, some business owners will roll the dice and not have the proper liability insurance on the business, medical insurance on themselves and their employees, key-man insurance, and business interruption insurance. What's more, legions of business owners expose their entire net worth to potential lawsuits because someone slips and falls on the premises, a worker becomes injured on the job, or something goes wrong with one of the company's products or services.

PROTECT YOUR FAMILY

Most business owners we work with are males, although we have worked with a sizable number of females, and that number will grow in the future. The wives of male entrepreneurs, more often than not, are also mothers. When it comes to their families, mothers are hard-wired to be security conscious. They are forever on the lookout for their children, their spouses, and for the lives that they have created.

If you're a married business owner, male or female, and your spouse has helped you over the years to create a lifestyle, how would you feel about having to tell your spouse that you could have cashed in and preserved your lifestyle, but you didn't?

Cashing in at the opportune moment has far greater ramifications than that which appears on a bank statement. I heard from an entrepreneur whose business went into the tank, the equivalent of losing it. He had had the opportunity to

> When you generate wealth the private equity way, you head down a path of lucrative and fulfilling rewards.

sell earlier for a huge amount but ignored it. When the business failed, his lifestyle and his wife's diminished. From then on, his relationship with his wife has not been the same.

We advise our clients to diversify in both domestic and international investments and establish a balanced portfolio of short-term and fixed investment vehicles, as well as private equity funds. If you are a high-net-worth individual, one of the soundest strategies for investing is to contribute to a fund of funds that invests in PEGs. That's where the returns are the highest. In essence, we would parlay our knowledge of PEGs, having been acquired by one, and use them as our investment vehicles.

When we work with business owners in preparation to sell the business, we help protect and defend them against all comers. Such protection is a critical component of the sales package, and we often focus on such activities first. In recent years, we've been advocates of deferred compensation programs, with strong death benefits for surviving family members. Such programs can be more affordable than you might presume.

For example, we worked with a sixty-year-old who was selling his business, and we were able to establish a powerful deferred compensation program for him. The compensation program serves as an integral part of a well-balanced portfolio. The individual is achieving a 15 percent return on investment, the average return that a fund of funds generates.

THE IMPORTANCE OF INTERMEDIARIES

When you're ready to sell your business, do so from an advantageous position. Make sure you have the best-qualified experts on your side, including an outstanding investment banker or intermediary, or both, who is experienced and knowledgeable about how acquirers value businesses. As I have been saying throughout this book, an intermediary is a key component in preparing your business for sale. Let me review the reasons.

First, most small business owners don't have the background, insights, or knowledge to directly approach or even find a buyer for their business, especially a PEG. Intermediary firms such as ours render a valuable service. We have the expertise and contacts to approach PEGs, and we have a deep database of potential acquirers in every industry.

Second, seasoned intermediaries have years of expertise in working with PEGs on transactions. As a result, we can tell you what a PEG will want from you. Armed with this information, you can make a high-quality first impression on a PEG and ease the transaction process.

> A sophisticated intermediary firm is going to find a way to optimize your opportunities with only a modicum of risk.

Third, it takes highly qualified experts to guide you through the labyrinth of tax laws that can affect the value you ultimately get from your business. Tax jurisdiction conflicts are tricky matters, for example. Also, we have seen a very large number of companies pay far more than necessary in taxes by basing their strategies on old tax law. Here's an example:

One of our clients was a construction business that was structured as a "C" corporation. He did not wish to buy back his shares in the company himself. However, because the tax laws had been changed in 1986, he was incurring double taxation. Moreover, owning the shares in his own company would have made the business much more attractive to a buyer.

Here's why: When buyers acquire stock, they incur two potentially costly disadvantages. First, they're stepping into the company's contingent liabilities, and second, they cannot depreciate, amortize, or expense the acquisition. Thus, their after-tax operating income is less, and the returns on the business investment prove to be less. So, they're only willing to pay so much for the company. In contrast, in an asset sale (with the company's stock counting as the owner's asset), all tangible and intangible assets (goodwill) are conveyed to the buyer.

Another of our clients was also using the "C" corporation structure to his disadvantage. We suggested that he change the company structure before going to market, and he agreed. It was a down year, not one in which you would want to sell, because the value of the company would be low. As he waited for a better time to sell, the company grew. The growth increased the company's value from $2 million to $9 million. And due to the structure change, this gain was taxed effectively at 20 percent (15 percent federal and 5 percent effective rate at the state level) for a tax burden of $1.4 million, instead of 50 percent, or $4.4 million. That represents $3.8 million in savings.

Companies across the country are incurring enormous financial suffering because they are structured improperly. Yet all of these businesses have accountants, tax attorneys, or other financial advisors. The problem is that these local advisors don't fully recognize or understand the issues here, and they fail to make the appropriate recommendations. We have seen time and time again that business owners are not receiving competent legal, tax, and accounting advice, at a devastating cost. The reason is simple: most accountants do not think about the eventual exit and its tax impact for their business owner and clients. This is not to condemn them—it's simply something to prepare for (another reason why long-term exit/transition planning is so critical).

I can't emphasize this enough: Local advisors may specialize in the preparation of income statements, balance sheets, and tax returns, but they have no expertise or don't view it as their responsibility to provide their clients with critical information about enhancing the value of their clients' businesses. That's why an advisor who understands how PEGs operate is critical.

The details associated with structuring an effective transaction can leave you in a disadvantaged position if you don't know precisely what you're doing. In the course of any business sale, there are many parties to the transaction. You could needlessly lose some portion of your equity, encounter thorny issues, and otherwise achieve less for the sale of your business. For these and so many other reasons, it is prudent to turn to the services of an intermediary to guide you in such transactions.

INTERVIEW: ON WORKING WITH INTERMEDIARIES

James Tilman (not his real name) has an interesting perspective on why a small business owner needs to work with an intermediary before preparing to sell the company to a PEG.

Bob: What is your background and your current practice?

James: Upon graduation, I spent twenty-five plus years with an international CPA firm rising to partner and then managing partner of an office. At forty-five, I decided to see if I could do what I'd been advising people to do for years. I founded a roll-up company in orthodontia and another company in plastic surgery.

I also served in a one-year stint as a dot-com CEO, where I built an organization and website with sixty-five thousand products. It was nearly cash-flow positive when the dot-com bubble burst and a $10 million commitment we had for funding evaporated on us, so we shut her down.

I then spent a year with a politician, seeking to develop a mezzanine fund that was for sale. First Union ran our capital source, but we couldn't raise that fund. The premise for our fund was that a former political figure with good connections would make investments in the companies that had business with the government. Through political advocacy, we would drive revenues to our portfolio companies. During that process, we had an ordinance removal company under contract that was represented by your firm. That's when I met you and one of your senior executives. We had supporting investors, but another company with a business model similar to ours experienced a scandalous period, and our investors were scared away.

Then I was employed by your firm. For three years, I helped you manage investment bankers across the country. Next, I was approached by Vision, a registered broker dealer, and became an equity partner when a group of us bought the company. I wouldn't have had that opportunity without you. Over the last five years, I've been doing mergers and acquisitions (M&A) advisory work with Vision that's similar to what I did with you.

Bob: What is your typical deal size?

James: Our range is the $5 million to $100 million, but our average is around $35 million. We've had larger deals than $100 million, but at that size, someone on the board will recommend a branded firm. We work by non-refundable retainer, typically between $7,500 and $15,000 a month, depending on the size and complexity of the deal.

Bob: What percentage of the businesses you sell are acquired by PEGs?

James: A large percentage, although they frequently list the strategic buyer and indicate that they are a portfolio company of a PEG.

Bob: Why would a business owner want to sell to a PEG?

James: Most business owners we represent want an attractive offer. Although they start the process with concerns about taking care of their employees, when offers arrive, they pick the most financially attractive. I can't recall one where the seller didn't pick the most attractive offer.

In the current environment, many of those are from strategic buyers, whether or not they are backed by a PEG. Strategics have had several years of admirable results, and they've got good capital and good borrowing capacity. Years ago, PEGs offered higher valuations because they had more capital than the strategics. But in my experience, business owners don't say, "I'll take less money, because I think this buyer will be better to my employees."

Bob: What might the advantages be in selling a PEG, as opposed to a strategic?

James: You did a good job summarizing my view in the title of this book. (Author's note: the original title was "Private Equity Groups: Always Sellers...Invaluable Insights for Private Business Owners.") PEGs only buy companies with the expectation of selling. Whether it is in three, five, or seven years, the motivation is to increase value and sell their acquisitions, recoup your investment, and get a return on that cash. PEG managers are compensated in only two ways: by some percentage of the administrative fees that they charge their portfolio companies, and by an 80-20 split on realized gains.

So by definition, PEGs seek to sell their acquisitions, get paid, and turn a profit. Their motivations are to streamline the cost structure, using capital to expand the market. In the lower middle markets, they can augment what I call the "management" or "human capital" involved. Many PEGs have either advisors or operating partners with operational experience. A strategic buyer not owned by a PEG has a management team focused on the same issues, as well as earnings per share, short-term profitability, and keeping the engine going for their stock price.

Bob: So a publicly held strategic buyer might take a longer view?

James: Yes. Occasionally PEGs maintain long portfolio holding periods. Their funds have an investment strategy that if it's a good cash flow, with a solid return on invested money, they're not compelled to flip them. Some PEGs hold acquisitions for fifteen to twenty years, but that's the exception, not the rule.

Bob: Many owners have much of their net worth tied up in their company. If they take some chips off the table, they can diversify their net worth by putting some cash in the bank. What's your perspective on that?

133

James: In the lower middle market, it's 50-50 between those who 1) want to do a recap, take some money off the table, and then have carried interest or some future benefit, versus those who 2) are at the end of their business's life cycle. They'll want to work on an employment agreement or a consulting period during the transition, but then they'll seek a complete exit.

Bob: Any advice for a lower middle market company owner who wants to maximize the ultimate exit?

James: Let me flip that around: a CEO/owner who doesn't build any kind of a management team, who wants to make all of the decisions and not let his people grow and develop, minimizes his prospects. You lose good people when they're not allowed to have a meaningful role. You also limit the number of people interested in your company.

Owners who don't value good accounting and records systems do themselves harm. As part of due diligence, most PEGs and large strategic buyers want to know where your customer concentration is: what you're selling and to whom. If you're using distributors, they want to know the details. Business owners anecdotally might have that information, but it's not quantifiable. A potential buyer won't say outright, "I'm knocking your value down because I don't know where your sales are from or what your margins are." In my view, though, it's implicit in the valuation they put on the business.

Bob: Ah, key distinctions between how PEGs and private owners run a business. What else?

James: This ties into both: no one likes to pay taxes. Some companies have been overly aggressive in managing their business and minimizing tax. A lot of business owners don't realize that while you only pay 35 percent tax, if you knock your valuation down because of poor accounting and decisions, it creates a tone with a potential buyer. If people are overly aggressive with their taxes, it dictates how much you can trust them, and potential buyers will look askance at that.

Bob: Business information and technology are changing rapidly, so how does a business owner of a growing company weigh opportunities and risks? Look at what happened in 2008 and 2009 with the recession.

James: The ones who've survived and prospered looked ahead. The trade-off is always how much they want to change their personal lifestyle by investing funds in their future while enjoying the benefits of their labor. We see companies that spend more money on sales, marketing, or new product development. Over a long period of time, that might have enhanced their value, but the business owner made a conscious decision that he wanted an enhanced lifestyle during his working years. Companies behind the curve will suffer in the valuation, for technology or other reasons. They may not even sell.

Bob: To sustain an enterprise, it's necessary to reinvest on an ongoing basis?

James: Yes, whether it's capital expenditure or technology. When the US had a heavier manufacturing base, many successful companies who preferred doing it the old way invested in new capital expenditure or better manufacturing techniques.

Bob: Of course, they had to re-up and take the risk that the technology would pay off in the long run. So you're taking a risk no matter how you cut it.

James: I don't think you can avoid it. If you don't take some risk, you won't be around; it will be a moot point.

CHAPTER 7: MOVING ON AFTER THE SALE

Once you have successfully sold your business, what's next? As I discussed earlier, you may wish to stay on and manage your business, and if you've sold to a PEG, that may be what the group wants, too. If not, you have many options, from being an active participant on the company's board to taking it easy at home with the grandkids. It's important to spend some time thinking about what you really want from life, and it is vital to stay active.

KNOWING WHEN IT'S TIME

When business owners first launch a venture, ignorance is bliss. Owners don't fully understand the risks involved, but perhaps they had no choice. Maybe starting a business was the best alternative for making a living. While the business is growing, owners receive a desirable, personal psychic reward.

As owners become more successful, they gradually become concerned about holding onto what they have as opposed to growing the business. Their children are growing, perhaps getting ready for college, and other family needs and expenses have arisen. Understandably, owners are focused on maintaining economic security. During this time, the owners' living expenses undoubtedly

137

have increased as well. What's more, how they perceive their place in the world has changed.

Many need or want a bigger house, a better car, or healthy financial investments to feel accomplished and successful. As time passes, they have more to lose than when they started. This impacts their willingness to seize opportunities to grow the business and, more specifically, to be ready to sell.

Accomplished small business owners often have been high-achieving individuals throughout their lives. They're good at pursuing what they want. As time passes, their dreams expand. They anticipate that tomorrow will hold more opportunities than today and that they'll be better able to take advantage of those opportunities.

MASLOW'S HIERARCHY OF NEEDS

One day, the game changes. The reasons owners started and have maintained their businesses might now be different than the reasons they're still in the business. From wanting to provide security for themselves and their families, upon reaching that goal, their perspectives can change markedly. Following Maslow's "Hierarchy of Needs," when we've achieved self-actualization, we continue to grow, but in a new direction. At some point in our lives, we owe it to ourselves to slow down, take the measure of our success, and permit ourselves to be satisfied with our achievements.

New Chapter, New Challenges

If you've been fortunate enough to sell your business at a high multiple, you now face new challenges and must devise new objectives. Many owners face the challenge of diversifying their assets as well as investing them. Having a lot of cash to invest is not an easy undertaking. The world is filled with noise and distraction, amidst opportunities to take what you've earned and parlay that into much more. There are also many ways to lose what you have worked so hard to obtain.

Most of the business owners we've had the pleasure to assist founded their own companies and have always served as founder and president. Most started with little in the way of funds. Over time, they built up considerable personal net worth as well as equity in the company.

Personal net worth and equity in a company are separate and distinct items, but they are largely one and the same for small business entrepreneurs. Hence, most of an owner's net worth is in the company, not outside of it, and this has ramifications.

Staying Involved

Once a founder is no longer a CEO, he or she can still play a vital role in the affairs of the company as a board member. After all, the board member has knowledge, experience, and relationships that can help the newly installed CEO to succeed. Executives may come and go, but there is only one founder.

It is vital, however, that founders contribute in a positive way. Too often, they unwittingly serve as a negative element, resisting the objectives of the new CEO and rallying others to do likewise. In Wasserman's study of CEO succession in technology-based ventures, three out of eight founders departed completely from their companies when they were replaced. Only one in four assumed a managerial position below that of the new CEO. Two in five became the board's chair. In another study, focusing on high-growth companies, one in four left the company altogether, while two in four served on the board of directors in some capacity for a five-year stretch.

Serving on the board can assist founders in establishing new roles and responsibilities for themselves. For example, the founder who has high competence in finance, engineering, or marketing can use that expertise to focus on helping the company in that particular area so that the new CEO's burden is lessened. As the new CEO demonstrates his or her capabilities and value added to the business, the founder is more at ease about serving on the board and remaining positive about the transition.

From my perspective, founders who aptly serve on boards of the company they started provide a valuable service. Their historical knowledge of the inner workings of the company clearly surpasses that of all others. They have perspectives, insights, and personal contacts that can be invaluable to the new CEO and the emerging board.

Freed from the unrelenting task of running all aspects of the company, many are able to envision new possibilities that had not been previously explored or simply had not occurred to them. They might be able to identify operating efficiencies. They might see connections between parts of the company or members of the distribution channel that weren't evident previously. Indeed, the CEO who becomes a high-contributing board member can become invaluable to the company he or she originally created.

Keeping Active

Once your business is sold, you won't have a controlling interest in the company. Of necessity, you'll witness significant changes. You'll need to prepare yourself both mentally and emotionally for such changes. Adopt the view in advance that nothing is going to stay the same.

You want to be cognizant of the most important forthcoming changes and how they'll impact your participation. You don't necessarily need to know all the details of all the changes to come, but stay focused on the most important ones. Being prepared for such changes can increase the odds of a smooth transition on your part.

People who have been active throughout their careers but retire early often shorten their longevity unless they stay active in something that invigorates them. Many people do not know what to do in retirement, however, and business owners in particular are hit hard. As a group, they are not good candidates for retirement and are uncomfortable not heading up an enterprise. So, to take true advantage of selling, formulate plans for what comes next.

Interview: Have a Life After You Sell

Our firm sold Smith-Sharpe in 2007. This interview with the owner, Gary Moore, sheds light on how to "have a life" long after the big event.

Bob: PEGs are prepared from day one to sell the companies they acquire. They engage in strategies and tactics that are considerably different from those of business owners. Nevertheless, you were committed to the selling process.

Gary: Your firm helped me in part commit to that process. I had looked at acquisition, and at selling, but not seriously. You challenged me to think about it more. The challenge to me was, "When do you think you will be ready to do this? It doesn't sound like you are committed to doing anything right now." And I realized what I was afraid of looking at and what I wanted for my future, and that moved me further along to the point of committing to sell.

Bob: When we examine an owner being ready and the business being ready, those are two distinct issues. The business can be ready, but the owner might not be, for a variety of reasons. For example, if the owner has no life outside the business, then even though the company might be ready to sell, the owner cannot make that transition. No matter how he tries, he might not be able to overcome the obstacles, because he has nowhere to go.

Gary: Right. Nothing is attractive to him; there's nothing beyond the company. I didn't have that problem. My situation was a combination of business and personal issues, and I was stuck in the middle, trying to decide where I wanted to go and how long I wanted to be here.

I had been in the business for twenty-eight years before I began to think, "Okay, I need to get this business to a point where it can be sold, if I want that. And then what am I going to do with myself afterwards?" It came together as two separate, vital, intertwined issues.

Bob: Let's address the first issue: you being committed and knowing what you were working towards, what you were going to do post-closing. What was the thought process, and what did you think you were moving to, or from, or both?

Gary: I had been through family stuff with my father's management and his illness, and the other half-owner's illness and his son being in the business. After all that happened, I had to manage it and figure out what was going to happen overall.

Bob: You had to take over the company after the deaths of your father and his partner, and things didn't work out with his son being in the business.

Gary: Right. I had to do it informally and, eventually, formally. So, it was confusing: running a business where my family's stock was in my mother's hands after my father's death, and the other family's stock was in the hands of a fellow who was old, sick, and not active in the business. Then his son pulled out and didn't want to do anything more with the business.

From a personal standpoint, I wasn't unhappy; I didn't need to continue doing what I was doing. I started to think: do I want to do this for another ten years? And I had to be honest with myself and say, "No, I actually don't want to." I was addressing employment issues, supplier issues, insurance issues, and money issues. I found that I had to move beyond being an owner: I had done that enough.

I was more interested by family, friends, neighborhood community, church—all those things that had my attention, but my very divided and oftentimes meager attention. I was coming home at 7:15 every night, when I should have been home at 5:15. I was missing committee meetings at church. My desire was to give back a little. Plus, my daughter was entering her teenage years, my sons had gone away to college, and I had a young grandchild with whom I wanted to connect.

I wanted to "re-fire" instead of retire and to get things in order. That was kind of the personal motivation for selling the business. It was comforting knowing that I didn't have to do it alone and that I didn't have to wait ten years. I didn't want to leave it on my wife's platter if I were to die. It was time to figure it out and make the business ready. And you taught me a lot.

Bob: Thanks. You're the only client I can recall who gave us a gift post-closing.

Gary: The gifts that I have been given, as a humble individual who is a part of this whole process, continue to this day. Dick's wife makes really cool quilts, and when I retired, his wife made me the most wonderful quilt. It has my name on it, and I use it all the time. I didn't know how important and how precious that relationship was.

Bob: Before to going to market, you had to prepare yourself mentally for selling the business and for what you were going to be doing after the business.

Gary: As best I could, with some lack of definition. But I had certain ideas.

Bob: It is difficult to sell a business under the best of circumstances; we certainly ran into issues selling Smith-Sharpe. Did being prepared mentally help you overcome the obstacles to selling?

Gary: Yes and no. I had the motivation to get something done. Various activities had to be completed to reach the point where the business sold. I collected my thoughts along the way about what I'd do next. I set up a file called the "greenfile" in my desk in which to place cut-out articles and other information on potential opportunities for the future. I would think to myself, "I can examine these when I get a bit closer to being totally out of here."

I always liked Norman Vincent Peale and his organization, Guideposts. So when I got an email in my inbox about volunteering for that organization's phone line, I moved that message over to the greenfile folder. I did that with several other messages and continued to say, "Okay, these things might be opportunities after selling my business."

Bob: Fantastic. We business owners live our jobs 24/7 and become so focused, like horses with blinders on, that we're missing the world. When you find something that might be of interest, if you don't file the information, you'll lose it.

Gary: Right, you'll lose it if you don't have it in a file or on your computer. In the ten years before that, I probably had a manila folder to stick stuff in. I call such desires "cravings," and parts of them are "dreams." Some of them don't pan out, and that's okay.

I didn't want to always be a businessman, although I loved making a living that way, and I even enjoyed all the things I had to do to profitably build the business. But it wasn't going to be my full boat, or it would have been a lot harder to get out of it.

Bob: After the sale, did you return to the greenfile?

Gary: Yes, and I'm following through on most of the ideas, such as working with a group of fun people in "helping" service. I work two days and two half-days with the food shelter and community outreach group. That was in my greenfile.

I also figured out that I don't want to be on the committees; I want to take action, meet people, and play with the other volunteers—but don't sit me down in meetings again, where I'm going to have to write a plan. I want to get my body moving a bit, but not necessarily go to the racquet club or join a gym.

Family and friends are also vital. I continue to learn how important it is to connect, but not in the way I used to: by grabbing the phone at work and arranging something. I used to consider that my connection to my family for the day, which is different than actually listening and being a part of their lives. Same with friends.

Bob: From the financial perspective, is post-closing what you anticipated?

Gary: Yes. As far as the outcome from the sale, it's been what I was expecting. The benefit has been evident. There are tax consequences that are more detailed than I presumed, but at the same time, it's been nice to have 7 percent interest on the new owner's money. Of course, such opportunities don't come every day.

The benefit package was a good arrangement. The balloon was nice. I have to figure out what do with it now; it's safe. Overall, the business is doing well, and the employees are happy. I don't have to hold my head down when I visit. I am glad that they have jobs and are tackling new challenges, for which they'll get a bonus if they do well, and their regular salary if they don't.

Bob: I'm glad to hear the business is doing well. The new owner is doing okay?

Gary: He had a little slow-down for while, but now business is booming. We've stayed friends, and that's another thing to celebrate. I see him when he comes up once a year. They are in a much bigger building, have added a firebrick service business, have added three people to the payroll, and employ others for short-term work.

Bob: So they've grown the company since it was sold.

Gary: Yes, they have, and it's been great timing. In fact, the sale has been good for everyone.

Conclusion

If you've made it this far, congratulations; you're quite serious about improving your business.

Assuming you've decided to implement several of the strategies suggested here, a suggestion may be helpful.

Select two easy steps to take and two longer term, higher value strategies that you work on simultaneously. In this way, it will be relatively easy to implement the former, and your success in doing so will provide you positive feedback, enabling the implementation of the latter.

As an owner myself, I know how difficult it is to implement change. It's the most difficult obstacle to overcome.

You can do it. You've accomplished far greater goals by the mere fact that you're successful and still in business. Implementation of these strategies will increase **the incremental value** of your business by multiples of the cost (in dollar terms and your valuable time.)

Great good fortune to you...and thanks for reading this book. I hope that it produces great results for you, because you deserve it.

Further Reading

Beckwith, Harry. *Selling The Invisible: A Field Guide to Modern Marketing.* New York: Business Plus, 1997.

Cook, Rupert. *Selling Your Technology Company for Maximum Value: A Comprehensive Guide for Entrepreneurs.* New York: Harriman House, 2011.

Covey, Steven, PhD. *The 7 Habits of Highly Effective People.* New York: Free Press, 2004.

Deans, Thomas William. *Every Family's Business.* Orangeville, Ontario: Detente Financial Press, 2008. http://www.everyfamilies-business.com/

Demaria, Cyril. *Introduction to Private Equity.* Hoboken: Wiley, 2010.

Evans, Frank, and Chris Mellen. *Valuation for M&A: Building Value in Private Companies.* Hoboken: Wiley, 2010.

Finkel, Robert. *The Masters of Private Equity and Venture Capital.* New York: McGraw-Hill, 2009.

Garson, Jack. *How to Build a Business and Sell It for Millions.* New York: St. Martin's Griffin, 2011.

Heslop, Andrew. *How to Value and Sell Your Business: The Essential Guide to Preparing, Valuing and Selling a Company for Maximum Profit.* London: Kogan Page, 2008.

Ittelson, Thomas. *Financial Statements: A Step-by-Step Guide to Understanding and Creating Financial Reports.* Pompton Plains, New Jersey: Career Press, 2009.

Kaplan, Steve. *Sell Your Business for the Max!* New York: Workman Publishing Company, 2009.

Laffer, Arthur, William Hass, and Shepherd Pryor. *The Private Equity Edge: How Private Equity Players and the World's Top Companies Build Value and Wealth.* New York: McGraw-Hill, 2009.

Leonetti, John. *Exiting Your Business, Protecting Your Wealth: A Strategic Guide for Owners and Their Advisors.* Hoboken: Wiley, 2006. (This is an excellent overview of how to prepare yourself and your business—both are equally critical—for an eventual exit. See the website also: http://www.exitingyourbusiness.com/)

Lipman, Frederick. *The Complete Guide to Valuing and Selling Your Business: A Step-By-Step Guide to Selling and Ensuring the Maximum Sale Value of Your Business.* New York: Prima Lifestyles, 2001.

Macarthur, Hugh, and Orit Gadiesh. *Lessons from Private Equity Any Company Can Use.* Cambridge MA: Harvard Business School Press, 2008.

Murray, Nick. *Simple Wealth Inevitable Wealth: How You and Your Financial Advisor Can Grow Your Fortune in Stock Mutual Funds.* The Nick Murray Company, 1999.

Prisciotta, Daniel. *Defend Your Wealth: Protecting Your Assets in an Increasingly Volatile World.* Ramsey, New Jersey: Prisco Publishing, LLC, 2011.

Richards, Rene. *How to Buy and/or Sell a Small Business for Maximum Profit—A Step-By-Step Guide.* Ocala: Atlantic Publishing Company, 2006.

Robb, Russell. *Selling Your Business: How to Attract Buyers and Achieve the Maximum Value for Your Business.* Holbrook: Adams Media Corporation, 2002.

Robbins, Doug. *There's Always a Way to Sell Your Business: 100 Tales from the Trenches by a Master Intermediary.* Toronto: BPS Books, 2010.

Siegel, Peter. *Businesses For Sale: How to Buy or Sell a Small Business––A Guide for Business Buyers, Business Owners, & Business Brokers.* Dublin OH: Siegel, 2005.

Slee, Robert. *Private Capital Markets: Valuation, Capitalization, and Transfer of Private Business Interests.* Hoboken: Wiley, 2011.

Trottier, Richard. *Middle Market Strategies: How Private Companies Use the Market to Create Value.* Hoboken: Wiley, 2009.

Warrillow, John. *Built to Sell: Creating a Business That Can Thrive Without You.* New York: Portfolio Hardcover, 2011.

Wasserman, Noam, PhD. "The Founder's Dilemma." *Harvard Business Review*, February 2008.

GLOSSARY OF TERMS

ACTUAL CASH VALUE: The value of an entity expressed in terms of cash or its exact and immediate equivalent. May be the same as "market value," depending on the applicable definition of the latter.

ADJUSTED BOOK VALUE: The book value that results after one or more asset or liability amounts are added, deleted, or changed from the respective book amounts.

AESTHETIC VALUE: The intangible, sometimes psychic, enhancement of value of an asset or asset group as a result of aesthetic factors or considerations. Examples include physical attractiveness that goes beyond functional requirements. Although frequently subjective in nature, aesthetic value can contribute to the economic value of property.

AMENITY VALUE: That portion of value that results from benefits or satisfactions enjoyed by the owner or user of property but that is not in the form of money or convertible to monetary terms. Amenity value tends to be subjective and is sometimes closely related to aesthetic value.

APPRAISAL: (Noun) The act or process of estimating value; an estimate of value. (Adjective) Of or pertaining to appraising and related functions, e.g. appraisal practice, appraisal services. It is synonymous with valuation.

APPRAISAL APPROACH: A general way of determining value using one or more specific appraisal methods. (See ASSET-BASED APPROACH, MARKET APPROACH, and INCOME APPROACH definitions.)

APPRAISAL DATE: The date as of which the appraiser's opinion of value applies.

APPRAISAL METHOD: Within approaches, a specific way to determine value.

APPRAISAL PRACTICE: The work or services performed by appraisers, defined by three terms in these standards: appraisal, review, and consulting.

APPRAISAL PROCEDURE: The act, manner, and technique of performing the steps of an appraisal method.

APPRAISED VALUE: Value as determined or estimated by an appraiser, particularly one acting on behalf of a governmental authority. The term appraised value is most often used in connection with real property and those types of personal property whose ownership is subject to taxes levied by local taxing jurisdictions. Appraised value may be based on market value or on some other basis appropriate to the type of property and to the applicable tax statutes, regulations, and customs.

ASSESSED VALUE: Value as established by governmental authorities as basis for taxation of property ownership. Usually synonymous with appraised value. In some jurisdictions, however, assessed value is a different (usually lower) figure than appraised value, depending on practices, procedure, and legal requirements that vary from jurisdiction to jurisdiction, from time to time, etc.

ASSET-BASED APPROACH: A general way of determining a value indication of a business's assets or equity interest, or both, using one or more methods based directly on the value of the assets of the business less liabilities.

BOOK VALUE: (1) With respect to assets, the capitalized cost of an asset less accumulated depreciation, depletion, or amortization as it appears on the books of account of the enterprise. (2) With respect to a business enterprise, the difference between total assets (net of depreciation, depletion, or amortization) and total liabilities of an enterprise as they appear on the balance sheet. It is synonymous with net book value, net worth, and shareholders' equity.

BUSINESS APPRAISER: A person who by education, training, and experience is qualified to make an appraisal of a business enterprise or its intangible assets, or both.

BUSINESS ENTERPRISE: A commercial, industrial, or service organization pursuing an economic activity.

BUSINESS VALUATION: The act or process of arriving at an opinion or determination of the value of a business enterprise or an interest therein.

CAPITALIZATION FACTOR: (1) The conversion of income into value. (2) The capital structure of a business enterprise. (3) The recognition of an expenditure as a capital asset rather than a period expense.

CAPITAL STRUCTURE: Any multiple or divisor used to convert income into value.

CASH FLOW: Net income plus depreciation and other non-cash charges.

CASH FLOW ANALYSIS: A study of the anticipated movement of cash into or out of an investment.

CLIENT: Any party for whom an appraiser performs a service.

COMMERCIAL VALUE: (1) The potential economic value of property if put to its most intensive and productive ("highest and best") use. (2) The present worth of future earnings and benefits. According to this definition, commercial value implies consideration of the effect of future happenings on the economic potential of an asset.

CONDEMNATION VALUE: Term sometimes applied to value for condemnation purposes. Condemnation value is not ordinarily a separate value as such; rather, value for condemnation purposes is most often a form of market value.

CONSULTING: The act or process of providing information, analysis of real estate data, and recommendations or conclusions on diversified problems in real estate, other than estimating value.

CONTRIBUTORY VALUE: The increment of value that an improvement or addition adds to an asset or group of assets. Term used primarily in connection with real estate valuation and appraisal.

CONTROL: The power to direct the management and policies of an enterprise.

CONTROL PREMIUM: The additional value inherent in the control interest, as contrasted to a minority interest, that reflects its power of control.

DEPRECIATED (BOOK) VALUE: Original cost of an asset less total amount charged as depreciation since the asset was acquired or created.

DEPRECIATED REPLACEMENT VALUE: Form of replacement value. The value of a thing as based on the (estimated) cost of replacing it with another thing of similar kind and condition (utility), explicitly taking depreciation of the thing being replaced into account.

DISCOUNT RATE: A rate of return used to convert a monetary sum, payable or receivable in the future, into present value.

EBITDA: Earnings Before Interest, Taxes, Depreciation, Amortization. This is the measure by which the profitability of most companies is evaluated. Said another way, revenue, less costs of goods, less normal operating income inclusive of a manager's market based compensation, before taxes, before depreciation, interest, and amortization.

ECONOMIC LIFE: The period over which property may be profitably used.

ECONOMIC VALUE: That kind of value according to which a thing (asset) is capable of producing economic (monetary or equivalent) benefits for its owner or user.

ENTERPRISE: See BUSINESS ENTERPRISE.

EQUITY: The owner's interest in property after deduction of all liabilities.

ESTABLISHED BUSINESS VALUE: Same as GOING CONCERN VALUE.

EXCESS VALUE: Value over and above market value. Term is usually confined to use in connection with real estate utilized for rental purposes, in which case excess value is the additional value attributable to a lease that guarantees rental income of an amount in excess of market rental at the time of appraisal.

157

EXCHANGE VALUE: Same as VALUE IN EXCHANGE.

FACE VALUE: Stated, or par, value of securities such as stocks, bonds, or the like, as set forth in the documents themselves.

FAIR MARKET VALUE: The amount at which property would change hands between a willing seller and a willing buyer when neither is acting under compulsion and when both have reasonable knowledge of the relevant facts.

FAIR VALUE: Same as FAIR MARKET VALUE, except usually no discount.

FEASIBILITY ANALYSIS: A study of the cost-benefit relationship of an economic endeavor.

FUNCTIONAL UTILITY VALUE: Somewhat obscure term generally implying a measure of the ability of a thing to provide usefulness, service, or profit.

GOING CONCERN: An operating business enterprise.

GOING CONCERN VALUE: (1) The value of an enterprise, or an interest therein, as a going concern. (2) Intangible elements of value in a business enterprise resulting from factors such as having a trained workforce, an operational plant, and the necessary licenses, systems, and procedures in place.

GOODWILL: The intangible asset that arises as a result of name, reputation, customer patronage, location, products, and similar factors that have not been separately identified or valued but that generate economic benefits.

GOODWILL VALUE: (1) Value attributable to goodwill. (2) The value of the advantages that a business has developed as a result of intangibles applicable to the specific business itself, such as name,

158

reputation, etc. (3) That part of the total value of a going enterprise that is in excess of the capital investment; an ingredient of going concern value.

INCOME APPROACH: A general way of determining a value indication of a business, business ownership interest, or security, using one or more methods wherein a value is determined by converting anticipated benefits.

INSURABLE VALUE: That portion of the value of an asset or asset group that is acknowledged or recognized under the provisions of an applicable loss insurance policy.

INTANGIBLE VALUE: Value of intangibles. Value not imputable to tangible assets.

INTRINSIC VALUE: Value inherent in a thing itself, as the metal content of a coin or article of precious metal jewelry. Term is subject to many possible interpretations and, therefore, requires extreme care in use.

INVENTORY VALUE: Term generally referring to the book value of the inventory of a business enterprise.

INVESTED CAPITAL: The sum of the debt and equity in an enterprise on a long-term basis.

INVESTMENT ANALYSIS: A study that reflects the relationship between acquisition price and anticipated future benefits of a real estate investment.

INVESTMENT VALUE: (1) Value as determined or estimated in accordance with the Investment Value ("income") Approach. (2) The value of a thing that arises from its presumed ability to produce a profit, or return on investment, for its owners. (3) Value to a particular investment or based upon individual investment requirements as distinguished from market value, which is value to a broader market than a single investor.

IRS FAIR MARKET VALUE: Not actually a single definition of value but rather a number of different definitions, similar in importance, that have been variously attributed to or used or accepted by the US Internal Revenue Service. Most or all of these definitions of IRS Fair Market Value include these elements: "Price at which property would change hands...between a willing buyer and a willing seller...neither being under any compulsion...both having knowledge of relevant facts..."

JUST VALUE: Term most often used in real estate appraisal. Generally considered to be synonymous with fair market value.

LEASEHOLD VALUE: The value of a leasehold interest, particularly in real estate appraisal.

LIQUIDATION VALUE: The (estimated) proceeds, net after provision for applicable liabilities, if any, that would result from sale of an asset or a group of assets if sold individually and not as part of the business enterprise of which they were originally a part. Sale may involve either forced liquidation or orderly disposal, with the amount of the net proceeds likely different for the two situations.

MAJORITY: Ownership position greater than 50 percent of the voting interest in an enterprise.

MAJORITY CONTROL: The degree of control provided by a majority position.

MARKET ANALYSIS: A study of real estate market conditions for a specific type of property.

MARKET APPROACH: The market approach is a general way of determining a value indication of a business, business ownership interest, or security using one or more methods that compare the subject to similar businesses, business ownership interests, or securities that have been sold.

MARKET VALUE: Market value is the major focus of most real property appraisal assignments. Both economic and legal definitions of market value have been developed and refined. A current economic definition agreed upon by federal financial institutions in the United States of America is:

The most probable price that a property should bring in a competitive and open market under all conditions requisite to a fair sale, the buyer and seller each acting prudently and knowledgeably, and assuming the price is not affected by undue stimulus. Implicit in this definition is the consummation of a sale as of a specified date and the passing of title from seller to buyer under conditions whereby:

1. buyer and seller are typically motivated;

2. both parties are well informed or well advised and acting in what they consider their best interests; a reasonable time is allowed for exposure in the open market;

3. payment is made in terms of cash in United States dollars or in terms of financial arrangements comparable thereto; and the price represents the normal consideration for the property sold unaffected by special or creative financing or sales concessions granted by anyone associated with the sale.

Substitution of another currency for United States dollars in the fourth condition is appropriate in countries or in reports addressed to clients from other countries.

Persons performing appraisal services that may be subject to litigation are cautioned to seek the exact legal definition of market value in the jurisdiction in which the services are being performed.

MARKETABILITY DISCOUNT: An amount of percentage deducted from an equity interest to reflect lack of marketability.

MASS APPRAISAL: The process of valuing a universe of properties as of a given date utilizing standard methodology, employing common data, and allowing for statistical testing.

MASS APPRAISAL MODEL: A mathematical expression of how supply and demand factors interact in a market.

MINORITY INTEREST: Ownership position less than 50 percent of the voting interest in an enterprise.

MINORITY DISCOUNT: The reduction from the pro rata share of the value of the entire business that reflects the absence of the power of control.

MORTGAGE VALUE: Value of an asset for mortgage borrowing purposes.

NET ASSETS: Total assets less total liabilities.

NET INCOME: Revenue less expenses, including taxes.

NET PRESENT VALUE: In investment theory, the difference between the cost of an investment, including improvements, and the discounted present value of all anticipated future benefits from that investment.

NET REALIZABLE VALUE: Same as LIQUIDATION VALUE.

NON-IDENTIFIABLE INTANGIBLE VALUE: Synonym for GOODWILL VALUE.

NUISANCE VALUE: In appraising, the price that would probably be paid for the avoidance of, or relief from, an objectionable condition or situation.

PERSONAL PROPERTY: Identifiable portable and tangible objects that are considered by the general public as being personal, e.g., furnishings, artwork, antiques, gems and jewelry, collectibles, machinery and equipment; all property that is not classified as real estate.

POTENTIAL VALUE: Value, or an increment thereof, that is dependent on the actual occurrence of stated possibilities or probabilities.

PRESENT VALUE: In investment theory, the current monetary value, frequently in the sense of the current value of future benefits. Discounted value of aggregate future payments.

RATABLE VALUE: That portion of the total value of an asset or asset group that is represented by the ownership interest of each of several owners. Could also be called pro-rata value.

RATE OF RETURN: An amount of income realized or expected on an investment, expressed as a percentage of that investment.

REAL ESTATE: An identified parcel or tract of land, including improvements, if any.

REAL PROPERTY: The interests, benefits, and rights inherent in the ownership of real estate. (Note: In some jurisdictions, the terms real estate and real property have the same legal meaning. The separate definitions recognize the traditional distinction between the two concepts in appraisal theory.)

REAL VALUE: (1) Synonym for MARKET VALUE. (2) True value of property whose owner may regard it as being worth more or less than it is actually worth.

REALIZABLE VALUE: Same as ADJUSTED BOOK VALUE.

RENTAL VALUE: Particularly in real estate, the monetary income reasonably expectable in return for the right to utilize property in an agreed manner.

REPLACEMENT COST NEW: The current cost of a similar new item having the nearest equivalent utility as the item being appraised.

REPLACEMENT VALUE: (1) The value of a business, asset, or asset group as determined or estimated by the Replacement Cost Approach. (2) Value as determined on the basis of the estimated cost of replacing the asset in question with other items of like kind and condition, and capable of producing equivalent benefits (results) for the user. Replacement value can be either depreciated replacement value or replacement value new.

REPORT: Any communication, written or oral, of an appraisal, review, or analysis; the document that is transmitted to the client upon completion of an assignment. (Note: Most reports are written, and most clients mandate written reports. Oral report guidelines [See Standards Rule 24] and restrictions [see Ethics Provision: Record Keeping] are included to cover court testimony and other oral communications of an appraisal, review, or consulting service).

REPORT DATE: The date of the report. May be the same or different than the APPRAISAL DATE.

REPRODUCTION COST NEW: The current cost of an identical new item.

REVIEW: The act or process of critically studying a report prepared by another.

RULE OF THUMB: A mathematical relationship between or among a number of variables based on experience, observation, hearsay, or a combination of these, usually applicable to a specific industry.

SALVAGE VALUE: The value in event of sale for scrap or similar purposes of property that has become uneconomic or useless for other purposes, of whose use for other purposes has been, or is to be, discontinued. Similar to, but not necessarily the same as, SCRAP VALUE.

SCRAP VALUE: The value of an article or articles in event of sale for removal and reclamation of the material of which the article is composed. Similar to, but not necessarily the same as, SALVAGE VALUE.

SENTIMENTAL VALUE: "Value" arising from an emotional relationship between a person (usually the owner) and a thing. Not ordinarily a form of economic value.

SOUND VALUE: In appraising, depreciated cost for (fire) insurance purposes.

SPECIAL PURPOSE VALUE: Value of a thing as related to its use for a special purpose, and that would not exist or would be substantially less if the thing were used for some other purpose.

SPECULATIVE VALUE: Synonym for POTENTIAL VALUE.

STABILIZED VALUE: In appraising, a value figure or estimate that excludes consideration of transitory conditions, such as abnormal relations between supply and demand, unusual and presumably temporary fluctuations in the cost of materials or labor, or the like.

SUBJECTIVE VALUE: (1) Value as related primarily or substantially to a state of mind.

(2) The value of a thing as based on or related to its ability to satisfy desires or wants (as distinct from needs). Subjective value is also sometimes called personal value.

TANGIBLE VALUE: The value associated with or attributable to tangible assets, such as land, buildings, machinery, furnishings, inventory, cash, and other assets that are susceptible to the senses.

TAXABLE VALUE: Same as ASSESSED VALUE.

UNIT VALUE: Value of an asset or group of assets expressed in terms of a unit of measurement of the quantity of the asset in question.

USE VALUE: Same as VALUE IN USE.

USER-IN-POSSESSION VALUE: (1) Synonymous with VALUE IN PLACE. (2) May include, in addition to value in place, value that may result from special use by the existing user, resulting in total value greater than that to any other user or potential user.

UTILITY VALUE: Generally a synonym for VALUE IN USE.

VALUATION: See APPRAISAL.

VALUATION RATIO: A factor wherein a value or price serves as the numerator, and financial, operating, or physical data serve as the denominator.

VALUE: The quality of a thing according to which it is thought of as being more or less desirable, useful, estimable, or important. The true "worth" of a thing according to some standard of worth.

VALUE AFTER THE TAKING: In condemnation proceedings, the value of the remaining portion of a formerly integrated or unified asset or asset group, after taking a part of the whole through condemnation proceedings.

VALUE BEFORE THE TAKING: In condemnation proceedings, the value of an integrated or unified asset or asset group, part of which is to be taken through condemnation proceedings.

VALUE IN EXCHANGE: (1) Value resulting from the quality of a thing such that it can be exchanged ("sold") for something else of monetary or equivalent value. Distinct from VALUE IN USE. (2) Market value as determined by comparison of the thing being appraised with other comparable things, particularly when the subject thing and the comparable thing fit the description of general purpose items, as opposed to single use or special purpose items.

VALUE IN PLACE: Value of an asset, such as machinery and equipment, that is already installed and ready for use, such as in a factory.

VALUE IN USE: (1) Value resulting from the quality of a thing such that its use can produce economic benefits for its owner or user. Includes value arising from the fact that the asset is already in place and operating. Sometimes different from VALUE IN EXCHANGE. Also termed utility value. (2) Market value of a special-purpose asset that has only a single use and, therefore, has a very limited market value to other than the current user.

VALUE TO OWNER: The special value of a thing to its owner, in that it suits his or her specific needs and requirements uniquely. (May sometimes include SENTIMENTAL VALUE).

WORKING CAPITAL: The amount by which current assets exceed current liabilities.

PRINCIPAL SOURCES

Real Estate Appraisal Terminology, edited by Byrl N. Boyce. American Institute of Real Estate Appraisers. 1975.

Business and Securities Valuation, by George Ovens and Donald I. Beach. Methuen Publications. 1972.

Canada Valuation Service, by Ian R. Campbell. Richard DeBoo Limited.

Webster's New World Dictionary, The World Publishing Co. 1958.

American Society of Appraisers, Business Valuation Standard. BVS-I, '2009

Uniform Standards of Professional Appraisal Practice, The Appraisal Foundation, Definitions – '2010

Appendix A: Resources

Private Equity Associations

The Private Equity Growth Capital Council - www.pegcc.org
An advocacy, communications, research, and resource center for and about PEGs and the industry

Association for Corporate Growth - www.acg.org
Includes professionals from private equity firms, corporations, and lenders who invest in middle-market companies

Emerging Market Private Equity Association - www.empea.net
A global body dedicated to an optimistic future for emerging private equity investment markets

Private Equity Association - www.peassociation.org
A professional organization for young private equity professionals in Boston, Chicago, and Los Angeles

Private Equity Chief Financial Officer Association - www.private-equitycfo.org
For individuals who manage the financial and operational aspects of private equity and other funds

BUSINESS ACQUISITION

Acquisition Central - www.acquisition.gov
More efficient and transparent practices through better use of information, people, processes, and technology

Business Acquisition & Merger Associates - www.buysellyourbusiness.com
A results-oriented, middle-market intermediary firm that helps clients acquire or sell companies

International Business Brokers Association - www.ibba.org
Formed to meet the needs of people and firms engaged in business brokerage and mergers and acquisition

PrivateEquity.com - www.PrivateEquity.com
An online directory of information and links, and an industry event calendar for venture capitalists, buyout firms, investment bankers, mergers and acquisitions groups, institutional investors, and consultants.

BUSINESS VALUATION

American Society of Appraisers Business Valuation - www.asabv.org
Accrediting society for appraisers with valuation expertise

Business Valuation - www.business-valuation.net
An online guide to business valuation

Business Valuation Resources - www.bvresources.com
Offers products and services for business valuation professions

Fair Market Valuations - www.fairmarketvaluations.com
The nation's largest infrastructure of business valuation consultants

Valuation & Information Group - www.valinfo.com
Offers valuation and financial consulting

Appendix B: Due Diligence

The following is a checklist of information and documents adapted from FindLaw® that you can expect the acquirer will want to review.

Organization, Incorporation, and Professional Standing

- Your company's articles of incorporation, bylaws, and all amendments

- Your company's organizational chart

- Your company's minute book, including all minutes and resolutions of shareholders and directors, executive committees, and other governing groups

- Your company's list of shareholders and number of shares held by each

- A Certificate of Good Standing from the Secretary of State where incorporated

- Copies of agreements relating to options, voting trusts, warrants, puts, and calls

- Copies of agreements relating to subscriptions and convertible securities

- Annual reports for the last three years

- Copies of active status reports in the state of incorporation for three years

- The list of states where the company is authorized to do business

- The list of all states, provinces, or countries where the company owns or leases property, maintains employees, or conducts business

- A list of all of the company's assumed names and copies of registrations

- Copies of any governmental licenses, permits, or consents

- Any documents relating regulatory agency proceedings related to the company

Financial, Revenue, and Tax Data

- Audited financial statements and the auditor's report for the last three years

- Most recent unaudited statements, with the prior year's comparable statements

- Auditor's letters and replies for the past five years

- Description of depreciation and amortization methods over the past five years

- Your company's credit report

- Projections, capital budgets, and strategic plans

- Analyst reports, if available

- A schedule of all indebtedness and contingent liabilities

- A schedule of accounts receivable and accounts payable

- Analysis of fixed and variable expenses and of gross margins

- The company's general ledger, including a complete roster of inventory

- A description of your company's internal control procedures

- Federal, state, local, and foreign income tax returns for the last three years

- Employment tax filings for three years

- State sales tax returns for the last three years

- Any audit and revenue agency reports

- Any tax settlement documents or excise tax filings for the last three years

- Any tax liens

REAL ESTATE AND PHYSICAL ASSETS

- A schedule of your company's business locations

- Copies of all real estate leases, deeds, mortgages, and title policies

- Copies of all property surveys, zoning approvals, variances, or use permits

- A schedule of fixed assets and their locations

- All UCC filings

- All leases of equipment

- A schedule of sales or purchases of capital equipment for the last three years

INTELLECTUAL PROPERTY

- A schedule of domestic and foreign patents and patent applications

- A schedule of trademark and trade names

- A schedule of copyrights

- Any patent clearance documents

- A description of important technical know-how

- A description of methods used to protect trade secrets and know-how

- Copies of "work for hire" agreements

- A schedule and copies of all consulting agreements, agreements regarding inventions, licenses, or assignments of intellectual property to or from the company

- A schedule and summary of any claims or threatened claims by or against the company regarding intellectual property

EMPLOYEES AND EMPLOYEE BENEFITS

- A list of employees, including positions, current salaries, salaries and bonuses paid during last three years, and years of service

- Resumes of key employees

- Copies of collective bargaining agreements, if any

- Copies of employment, consulting, non-disclosure, non-solicitation, or non-competition agreements between the company and any of its employees

- Personnel handbook and a schedule of all employee benefits and holiday, vacation, and sick leave policies

- Summary descriptions of qualified and nonqualified retirement plans

- A description of all employee problems within the last three years, including alleged wrongful termination, harassment, and discrimination

- A description of any labor disputes, requests for arbitration, or grievance procedures currently pending or settled within the last three years

- A list and description of benefits of all employee health and welfare insurance policies or self-funded arrangements

- A description of worker's compensation claims history

- A description of unemployment insurance claims history

- Copies of all stock option and stock purchase plans and a schedule of grants

ENVIRONMENTAL IMPACTS (IF APPLICABLE)

- A roster of environmental permits and licenses

- Environmental audits, if any, for all properties that you lease or manage

- A roster of hazardous substances your company handles

- A description of your company's disposal methods

- Copies of all EPA, state, or local regulatory agency correspondence and files

- A roster identifying and describing any environmental litigation or investigations, Superfund exposures, contingent environmental liabilities, or indemnification obligations

CONTRACTS, AGREEMENTS, AND RETAINED ADVISORS

- A schedule of all subsidiary, partnership, or joint venture relationships and obligations, with copies of all related agreements

- Copies of all contracts between the company and any officers, directors, five-percent shareholders, or affiliates

- All loan agreements, bank financing arrangements, lines of credit, or promissory notes to which the company is a party

- All security agreements, mortgages, indentures, collateral pledges, and similar agreements, including guaranties to which the company is a party, and any installment sale agreements

- A roster of all law firms, accounting firms, consulting firms, and similar professionals engaged by the company during the past five years

- All distribution agreements, sales representative agreements, marketing agreements, and supply agreements

- All letters of intent, contracts, and closing transcripts from mergers, acquisitions, or divestitures within last five years

- Options and stock purchase agreements involving interests in other companies

- Your company's standard quote, purchase order, invoice, and warranty forms

- All nondisclosure or noncompetition agreements impacting the company

- All other contracts and agreements

PRODUCTS AND SERVICES

- A list of existing products or services and those products or services under development

- Reports and documents related to regulatory approvals or disapprovals of company products or services

- A summary of all complaints or warranty claims

- A summary of results of all tests, evaluations, studies, surveys, and other data regarding existing products or services and products or services under development

CUSTOMERS OR CLIENTS

- A roster of the company's largest clients or customers over the last three years

- All supply or service agreements

- The company's purchasing policies

- The company's credit policy

- A list of unfilled orders

- A list and explanation for any major customers lost over the last three years

- All market research reports and surveys relevant to the company or its products or services

- The company's current advertising programs, marketing plans, and budgets

- A sample of each of the company's printed marketing materials

- Descriptions of the company's major competitors

- Copies of all articles and press releases relating to the company within the past three years

INSURANCE, LEGAL PROTECTION, LITIGATION

- A copy of general liability, personal and real property, product liability, errors and omissions, key-man, directors and officers, worker's compensation, and other insurance

- A schedule of the company's insurance claims history for the past three years

- A summary of all pending, threatened, and past litigation

- Copies of insurance policies related to pending or threatened litigation

- Documents relating to settlements, injunctions, and consent decrees to which the company is a party

- A list of unsatisfied judgments

About the Author

Bob Scarlata is currently a member of Pinnacle Equity Solutions, which promotes exit planning for business owners throughout the US. A leader in the industry, he has helped hundreds of businesses handle the complex array of steps required to successfully sell a company for a multiple of its initial value. In the mid-1980s, Bob founded and led a privately held mergers and acquisition firm specializing in the marketing and sale of closely held businesses throughout the United States and Canada. He has also held sales and marketing positions in international manufacturing concerns. Bob holds a B.S. in Business Administration from the University of Connecticut and a J.D. from the University of Miami. He resides in Nashville with his wife, Rhonda. He can be reached at BScarlata@Corporations4Sale.com. 615-383-5222.

Made in the USA
Middletown, DE
18 March 2018